JUDGING THE JUDGES

Judging the Judges

JUSTICE, PUNISHMENT, RESISTANCE, AND THE MINNESOTA COURT DURING THE WAR IN VIETNAM

Kenneth E. Tilsen

NORTH STAR PRESS OF ST. CLOUD, INC.

Library of Congress Cataloging-in-Publication Data
Tilsen, Kenneth E., 1927-
　　Judging the judges : a study and commentary : looking at the
decisions of the Minnesota Federal District Court judges in
Selective Service cases during the Vietnam War / Kenneth E.
Tilsen.—1st ed.
　　　p. cm.
　　Includes bibliography, references, and index.
　　ISBN 0-87839-186-X (pbk. : alk. paper)
　　　1. Trials—Minnesota. 2. Draft resisters—Minnesota—History.
　　3. Draft—Law and legislation—United States—Criminal provisions
　　—History. 4. United States. District Court (Minnesota)—History.
　　I. Title.

KF221.P6 T55 2002
343.73′0122--dc21   2002069320

Printed in the United States of America by
Versa Press, Inc., East Peoria, Illinois.

Published by
North Star Press of St. Cloud, Inc.
P.O. Box 451
St. Cloud, Minnesota 56302

Dedication

To Rachel

Contents

Foreword ix

Introduction xi

Author's Note xix

Chapter One   Resisters Meet the Court 1

Chapter Two   The Draft 23

Chapter Three   Judging 31

Chapter Four   Judge Miles Lord 33

Chapter Five   Judge Edward J. Devitt 47

Chapter Six   Judge Larson 67

Chapter Seven   Judge Philip Neville 85

Chapter Eight   Denouncement 113

Afterwards   What Became of the Resisters? 129

Endnotes 147

Acknowledgments 183

Appendix 185

Selected Bibiography 231

Index 235

Foreword

American political debate from the time of the Constitutional Convention of 1787 down through the horrific days following the September 11, 2001, attacks on New York City and Washington, D.C., has always featured, at its core, the burning question Ken Tilsen asked in *Judging the Judges*: "What kind of country will we be?" This question of the national identity is surrounded by overtones of what justice means in America because the United States is a republic formed under law with freedom as its theme song. America is formed out of a love affair with the "equal liberty" embraced in the Declaration of Independence, rather than the ancient bonds of soil and blood. Thus, the question of national identity in America is presented in new forms, by new voices, in every generation. And each generation, in its own way, provides an answer for its time which can inform future generations as they come to face the same question in their time. At the Constitution Convention, and for much of the nineteenth century, the question of national identity often arose around the question of racial justice as the young nation struggled with the many issues surrounding the slave trade, slavery, and racial segregation. In the late twentieth century, the question of national identity at the heart of the debate over the nation's deep involvement in the undeclared war in Vietnam dominated the life of an entire generation, now beginning to grow old. Today, in the post-September 11, 2001, period, the question of national identity is being asked again as the nation struggles with questions that pit the America's old love of freedom against new threats to homeland security. In every one of these instances, for over two centuries, federal courts have been deeply involved in shaping the answers to the perennial question of national identity. Yet this phenomenon is rarely examined. What the late Robert Cover did in *Justice Accused,* his study of Northern abolitionist judges of the nineteenth century who steadfastly returned fugitive slave after fugitive slave to their owners, Ken Tilsen has done in *Judging the Judges,* his study of those federal judges of the Vietnam era of the twentieth century who reserved the harshest sentences for those anti-war and anti-Selective Service resisters who were most public and active in their resistance. As Tilsen demonstrates, when the freedom of those who most publicly and most actively sought public attention in an effort to expand the debate over American involvement in Vietnam was at stake, the judges retreated into a static and formalist view of law that left no room for the creative application of law that justice requires. Like the abolitionist judges of the past, the Vietnam-era judges acted in ways that tended to discourage, rather than promote, the kind of debate needed in each generation to answer the question: "What kind of country will we be?" The story Tilsen tells is a reminder of both the power and responsibility of the judicial branch to promote or subvert the effort of each generation to provide its answer. In the post-September 11th days, we have now entered, it should serve as a warning to the dangers that lie ahead as well as of the promise if we insist, as we must, that the only reason for the rule of law is to serve justice.

> Howard J. Vogel
> Professor of Constitutional Law and Jurisprudence
> Hamline University School of Law
> May 9, 2002

Introduction

T his book began primarily as an effort to remember and record a part of the least explored history of the Vietnam War era. Much has been written about the war, the opposition and resistance to the war, the breakdown of the Selective Service system, and indeed the massive disruption of the military. Hardly a day passes without a reminder of the continuing effects of the cultural divide that shook our nation.

The specific suggestion for a work on the Selective Service system came about when I dropped in on my oldest son's fiftieth birthday poker party. A number of his friends reminded me that I had helped them with draft-related problems during the Vietnam War. They began to tell their individual stories, ranging from indictments for refusal to report for induction; conscientious objector claims, military service stories and post-military horrors. Each recalled and related in some way their participation in Vietnam anti-war or anti-draft activities, and several suggested that I should write about my experiences in defending Selective Service indictments.

I graduated from the University of Minnesota Law School in 1950 and practiced law from offices in downtown St. Paul until I closed my office in 1994 and began teaching part time at the Hamline University School of Law. For the last thirty-five years of my practice, I spent the greatest part of my time representing and supporting Native Americans, Afro-Americans, farmers, workers, and peace and social justice activists as they worked to effect change in our society. And as they were arrested in the course of their work, I often found myself defending them against criminal charges before the state and federal courts. Thus, it was not surprising that I represented many young men charged with refusing induction or refusing to register during the course of the Vietnam War.

I did not particularly want to write about my experiences, but I did believe that what passed for commentary about the military draft and prosecutions under that law seemed ill informed. What was missing was some recognition of the role and importance of the federal trial judges. I took up the challenge to do a study upon which I would base my comments. Thus *Judging the Judges* was born.

A quarter-century after the last United States troops fled Vietnam, the war and its consequences continued to pervade the American psyche. In late July of 1999, PBS, the Public Broadcasting System, presented a new program discussing the history of our entry into the war in Vietnam based on the latest examination of presidential records. It was entitled: *Vietnam: Descent Into Hell—An American Tragedy.* At one point in the program, President Lyndon Johnson is heard to say that he has a man, a soldier with small children, working for him on his ranch in Texas. When he thinks of sending men to Vietnam, he questions what he would say to this man. What earthly reason could he give to him to explain why he must go to Vietnam? "I don't think it's worth fighting for."

Controversy over and opposition to the war in Vietnam brought down President Lyndon Johnson and contributed to President Richard Nixon's forced departure.

The year 2000 was widely memorialized as twenty-five years after the fighting ended in Vietnam. In television and newspaper special reports abounded, as well as books and articles. A list of all books and retrospective articles concerning the war written since 1975 would surely exceed a hundred pages. Among the most recent publications are *Legacies of Vietnam*, edited by Lawrence R. Velvel; *The Long View*, Volume 5, Number 3, Massachusetts School of Law, Summer 2001; *After Vietnam: Legacies of a Lost War*, Charles E. New (2000), John Hopkins University Press; *A Grand Delusion: Americas Descent into Vietnam*, Robert Mann, Basic Books, 2001; and "A Generation's Wounds Persist 25 Years Later," Michael Olesker, originally published by the *Baltimore Sun* and reprinted by the *Minneapolis Star Tribune* on November 27, 2000.

Chance and Circumstances: the Draft, the War, and the Vietnam Generation by Lawrence M. Baskin and William A. Strauss is the most important work that focuses on that part of the American people who were confronted most immediately with the reality of Vietnam, the twenty-seven million draft-age men who were the Vietnam generation. That work was based upon the "Vietnam Offender Study" conducted at the University of Notre Dame. Almost every subsequent publication relied upon that work for the basic nationwide data relating to the Vietnam generation and its insight into the significance of the material. The impact of the war on draft age men defined the lives of millions of Americans who are now nearing middle age. They faced at one extreme the horror of war and at the opposite extreme the vagaries of a judicial system holding out the specter of prison life.

The war in Vietnam presented the United States federal court system with the unprecedented crush of criminal indictments resulting from the reluctance of draft age men to participate in the war. As the war escalated and its unpopularity among the American public increased, the federal government was faced with over 200,000 apparent draft violators. Between 1965 and 1975 the federal government indicted 22,500 persons for draft law violations. Seven hundred seventy-eight of those persons were indicted in the State of Minnesota.

In 1972 over fifty percent of the total criminal case load of the Minnesota Federal Court represented Selective Service cases. These indictments were handled with only a few exceptions by four sitting federal judges: Judge Edward N. Devitt, Judge Earl R. Larson, Judge Phillip Neville, and Judge Miles W. Lord. These judges were remarkably dissimilar in political and social outlook, and each approached his judicial tasks from a different legal background and life experiences.

I knew the judges, and I knew the process. I tried over thirty-five Selective Service cases and probably handled at least that many more that were dismissed without trial. Of the judges who handled these cases, three are now deceased. Judge Larson died after I started writing this book. Judge Lord is retired from the bench but still active and available in the community.

I do not believe that the judges in Minnesota or the Minnesota anti-war and anti-draft movement or the political climate in Minnesota were so unique that the conclusions apply only to these judges. Certainly the judiciary in some states acted with greater punitive measures against those who violated the draft laws and in others more leniently. Likewise, anti-war sentiment in Minnesota was greater than in many states but surely not greater than California or the New England states. If we can, in fact, point to Minnesota as having a more populist political character or being more informed by a politically active professional or intellectual tradition, it only emphasizes the significance of the results. For, if the federal courts of "liberal" Minnesota can do no better than disclosed by the material in this book, the implications for other states are more ominous.

The cases that interested me corresponded with the war years and the draft: 1967 to 1974. This was before the computer era, and no effort had ever been made to catalogue cases by specific charges. The federal courts maintained separate docket books for criminal cases. These books were initially located in St. Paul, Minneapolis, and Duluth for all six of the divisions of Minnesota. Many of these books had been transferred to a federal depository in Chicago. Each relevant book for each year and for each six divisions had to be located and each page examined to determine if it involved a Selective Service violation.

Because of the nature of the process, I cannot be certain that my collection is absolutely correct with no omissions. I was concerned not only with the result in each case that could be obtained from the docket sheets but also the written memorandum of every contested case. This was an even more daunting challenge and involved the location of each case I identified as a possible source of a judicial memorandum. The opportunity for error in this search is apparent. Indeed a small number of requested files were never found.

I did locate and reference about 125 memoranda opinions by the four judges. While the data does disclose some clear differences in judicial behavior and sentences as well as differences in judicial attitudes, reasoning and process, I feel that readers will have a variety of opinions about the significance of each distinction. For myself the differences are far less pronounced than I would have expected.

The judicial system was near collapse from the weight of the draft related cases before the court. On July 30, 1972, there were 390 criminal cases pending in the Minnesota federal courts. Two hundred and fifty-three of those cases were Selective Service cases. Yet with few exceptions, the judges' decisions proceeded as if mention of the underlying reasons that brought the defendants before the court would violate some judicial code or rule of law.

I'm sure in many cases, perhaps most, the attorneys and defendants played their part. Defense of Selective Service cases became a kind of formalized dance—not a two-step, but a ritualized passage through an arcane set of statutes, regulations, rules, and memoranda. Jesuit or Talmudic training served one well. But often, especially to the resisters, young men determined to stop the war by their personal acts, the war was the only topic before the court. And here the court became the resister. It was clearly impolite to talk about the war. Moreover, to suggest to the court, as I did on occasion, that the judge consider his role directly was, in the word of at least one judge, "abrasive."

Yet, all four Minnesota judges, despite their general differences, reserved their most severe sentences for the defendants who had taken active steps to oppose the war or the Selective Service system. In so doing, they were following the lead, knowingly or not, of the Honorable Gus J. Solomon, chief judge of the United States District Court for the District of Oregon. Judge Philip Neville did in fact refer to Judge Solomon in connection with his sentences, but it is unclear if even Judge Neville recognized that he was following Judge Solomon's lead not only in almost always sentencing draft law violators to prison, but also in sentencing active war and draft resisters to the greatest sentences.

The record in Minnesota is unequivocal. Resisters, if they were motivated by opposition to the war to take open, public acts to oppose the war and the draft, could expect to get harsher punishment for any violation of the draft laws.

The point seems to be, the more one's motives were greater than personal desire to escape the draft, the more the motive included concern for others, the community, and the world, the greater would be one's personal penalty.

Most observers of our legal system subscribe to the oft-quoted words of Mr. Justice Holmes that the courts do not serve justice, they serve the law. But if the purpose of law is to do justice, how can that be right? And if it is right, should it be right?

I am indebted to Professor Howard Vogel, a friend and colleague at Hamline University School of Law who introduced me to the work of Robert Cover. In 1968 Cover, then a young assistant professor, wrote a book review published in the *Columbia Law Review*. The book reviewed was a reprint of an 1856 compilation entitled, *Atrocious Judges: Lives of Judges Infamous as Tools of Tyrants and Instruments of Oppression*. Cover took the occasion of the book review to write a polemic against the American judiciary. He compared the behavior of the federal courts in 1968 in convicting and sentencing draft resisters with the judges who enforced the Fugitive Slave Act in the pre-civil war era. He noted that while we generally do not seek moral guidance from our judges, the federal judiciary has remained faithful to its long tradition as executors of immoral laws. He decried the fact that:

No judge has resigned in protest. No judge has availed himself of the opportunity presented by a draft case to instruct the public on the moral issues of the war.

No judge has publicly engaged in creative judicial obstruction of the war effort. With Nazi Germany fresh in our minds, with the screaming silence of the German people barely passed into history, the silence and more, the cooperation of the federal bench demands comment.

It is that demand for comment that motivates this book.

Author's Note

On September 11, 2001, as airplanes used like guided missiles destroyed the Twin Towers of the World Trade Center in New York City, our country was shaken, and the political, intellectual and cultural landscape was changed as radically as the New York City skyline. The immediate effect of the September eleventh attacks was to reduce all other problems to relative insignificance. The images of the destruction and deaths were overpowering, too personal to permit other concerns to be noticed or survive. In the aftermath of the attacks, I thought this book might be abandoned. The ideas and concerns discussed here appeared so far removed from the public agenda that completing the project seemed self-indulgent. Would people still care about how the judges dealt with those who refused to fight a war they thought was wrong, immoral and illegal?

The War in Vietnam tore our country apart and appeared to destroy the social bonds that make us a nation. As our weapons exploded in a small country half way around the world, an image of that war imploded here. The War in Vietnam divided us. The initial effect of the September 11th attack brought us together in ways not seen since World War II.

Is there still something to be gained by looking at the actions of judges when faced with Vietnam-era draft resisters? I think there is much to be gained, for it is much more likely than not that the present apparent unity will not be long lasting. Sooner or later our courts will again be faced with making decisions affecting the lives of our people in a period of great division among us, and the courts' decisions will arise directly out of the issues that divide us. Before the Civil War, at a time when the issues of slavery were dividing the nation, the courts dealt with the fugitive slave laws with less than glorious results. After the Civil War, during and after World War I, in the midst of the Great Depression, following World War II, and in the course of the civil rights movement of the sixties, the courts faced a plethora of issues of great controversy in the context of a divided nation.

Others have and will continue to debate how well or badly the courts responded. But there is little doubt the courts will be called upon to act again in a period of internal strife. It is interesting to note that the unity forged in World War II was sustained, at times perilously, by the Cold War against world communism. It broke on the anvil of Vietnam less than twenty-five years after World War II ended. Unless there are substantial changes in government policies, it is unlikely that the war against terrorism will serve to unite us for that long.

As the images of September eleventh fade, we are faced with new realities, and many are alarmed by the actions of our government. Since September eleventh, the federal government has approved secret military tribunals for accused terrorists, given law enforcement unprecedented power to tap phones and read e-mail and helped foster an atmosphere of self-censorship spelled out by White House spokesman Art Fleischer, who warned Americans "to watch what they say."Arrests and detentions, suspension of habeas corpus, special courts, massive questioning of legal residents because of their ethnic background or religion—all this and to date a mostly silent public and silent judiciary. But concern over civil liberties is only the tip of the iceberg. We see developing an almost unprecedented effort to prevent the expression of any point of view that diverges from Washington orthodoxy, enforced by a frightenly omnipresent call to patriotism allegedly in service to those who lost their lives on September 11, 2001, and "our boys in uniform."

Not one to be left behind, Minnesota Governor Jesse Ventura jumped on the bandwagon and questioned the patriotism of members of the Minnesota legislature for not adopting his plan to solve the Minnesota budget deficit. In Washington, Senate Republican leader Trent Lott all but called Democratic Senate leader Tom Daschle a traitor for questioning the direction of the effort to destroy the Taliban. "How dare Senator Daschle criticize President Bush while we are fighting our war on terrorism especially when we have troops in the field? He should not be trying to divide our country while we are united."

The remarks of Governor Ventura may be ignored as ludicrous, but the statements of spokespersons for the administration and the Republican leader are ominous. President Bush has left little doubt that he expects to engage us in a war without end. Like the Vietnam War it is undeclared. It is a strange war against a foe without a nation but carries with it a threat to evolve into a war against any number of nations. At times it seems more like the "War on Drugs" or a political campaign in which the term "war" is a semantic device used for the purpose of raising emotions and support.

Semantic or not, we have a continuing war economy, in which the largest budget component for over sixty years is for past, present, and future wars. The president has presented a budget for this war that would raise our military budget by a whopping forty-eight billion dollars for a total of $396 billion, an eighty-seven-billion-dollar increase from when he took office in January 2001. Assistant Secretary of Defense (under Ronald Reagan) Lawrence Korb, speaking for Business Leaders for Sensible Priorities in opposition to the budget request, pointed out that this year's "increase of forty-eight billion dollars alone is more than the total military budgets of every nation in the world."

In addition to suppression of different views on the proper path to prevent future terrorist attacks, there is a growing indication that a fight is brewing to decide what kind of a country we will be. There is dismay that the proposed budget leaves little room for advances in our health, welfare, and education systems. Indeed, the initial response to the attacks was to propose huge tax reductions and give-aways to the wealthiest corporations and individuals in the country. Conservationists see the fight against terrorists being used as an excuse for destroying the conservation gains of the past and a fig leaf to cover up a scramble for profits by raiding the Alaska wilderness and other pristine lands. The unilateral withdrawal from international conventions, treaties, agreements, and conferences involving global warming, weapon and anti-missile control, chemical and biological warfare, and more, alarms most of the world and many here at home. The apparent change in our nuclear policy made without public discussion or debate that would have our country use nuclear weapons is certain to shock most of the world and many Americans.

The program announced by President Bush for an endless war against other nations and in particular Iraq has the potential to destroy the illusory unity in this country and once again turn America into a war within a war—not because Americans like Saddam Hussein and do not wish for a different government in Iraq but because of the probable consequences of a decision to take military action against Iraq. Among our major allies, France, Germany, and Russia have trade relations with Iraq and would not support military action. America would have no real allies in such a venture. Most of the world rejects our rationale for attacking Iraq, and the specter of a U.S.-Israeli war against Iraq would have the whole Arab-speaking world against us instead of just a religious fundamentalist sect of Muslim terrorists.

An attack on Iraq would require 200,000 to 300,000 troops for the invasion, 700 to 1,000 aircraft and one to five carrier battle groups. Such a force would raise the specter of reinstatement of the draft. It is more likely than not that we will see another period in our history when the courts will face a crisis in this country.

The experience of the federal courts during the Vietnam crisis is not a pretty picture. With that in mind, and because I believe we are laying the foundation for another divisive crisis in our nation, I did not abandon this book. I pushed to complete this work rather than abandon it after the September eleventh attacks to honor the memory of those young men who served our country well and went to prison in such service, because I believe that knowledge is power and change is possible, and in the hope that history does not have to repeat itself.

Kenneth Tilsen
March 2002

Chapter One

Resisters Meet the Court

David Pence

David Pence was dubbed the "Julie Andrews of the Resistance" by a Minneapolis newspaper. Short, rosy-faced, talkative, friendly, expansive—Pence was all of these.

Born and raised in Crystal, Minnesota, an old, blue-collar suburb of Minneapolis, Pence was the son of a proud World War II Marine veteran and a mother committed to giving her children a good Catholic education. Pence went to a Catholic boys' grade school and high school (Benilde), graduating in 1964, and then went to a Catholic seminary, Nazareth Hall. In 1966 he thought he wanted to become an urban priest, so he joined VISTA and moved to Wilmington, Delaware. His plan was to work in a black community and then come back to Minnesota. In high school he had been the editor of the school magazine and wrote in favor of a quick end to the Vietnam War. He described himself as being in the "Tom Dooley Camp," which meant that he believed that especially Catholics should resist communist encroachment in Vietnam. In New York, Pence stated that he "met the first Jewish or black guys in his life." He lived with them as they worked to organize rent strikes, and Pence soon became aware of and involved in questions of poverty and racial justice. He returned to St. Paul having given up not only his plan to be a priest but his belief in God.

Pence registered for the draft in 1964 at the seminary when he was eighteen. He was classified 4D (divinity student deferment). When he worked in the VISTA program, his selective service classification was changed to 2A (occupational deferment).

In VISTA, he became committed to non-violence first in that struggle and later as part of foreign policy. He became very opposed to the war in Vietnam, and, along with a roommate, filed for a conscientious objector classification in May of 1967.

Left to right: Francis Shor, Dave Pence, and Dave Gutknecht on the steps of the induction center in Minneapolis after Gutnecht refused induction. Shor and Pence had refused previously. (From the *St. Paul Dispatch-Pioneer Press* News Negative Collection. Courtesy of the Minnesota Historical Society)

2

About the same time Pence filed for a C.O., he was exposed to David Harris of Stanford and other draft resisters. Harris was one of the first persons Pence had met to publicly argue that if people wanted to stop the war in Vietnam, they shouldn't go off to work in a hospital and let those who didn't have that education or privilege go out to fight. David Gutknecht, Francis Shor, George Crocker, James Dombroski, and others were among the early leaders of the resistance movement in Minnesota, and they were also making that argument. Pence, along with ninteen-year-old Gutknecht and Shor, twenty-two, turned in their draft registration cards as part of an October 16, 1967, antidraft demonstration in Minneapolis and across the country. As a result, these three all were classified 1A and ordered to report for induction. Pence is quoted in the newspaper as saying that they would not accept conscientious objection status because "to do so would be to accept the other inequities in the draft system."

Dave Gutknecht

Dave Gutknecht was born in 1947 in Winthrop, Minnesota, a small rural community. His father was a World War II veteran. Both parents worked outside the home; they divorced when he was fourteen. He left high school after his junior year, moved to Minneapolis and started taking classes at Augsburg College in Minneapolis. In 1965/ 1966 he began taking courses at the University of Minnesota, became an active participant in antiwar teach-ins, read widely and got involved with local groups opposing the war.

Gutknecht registered for the draft when he turned eighteen and, shortly thereafter, advised his local board that he wanted to file as a conscientious objector. His C.O. request was not processed since he had a student deferment. Within the next year, he dropped out of school and did not advise his local draft board. Dave described himself as becoming more and more committed to resisting participation in the war. He began working with draft-age men in 1967 and, in August and September of that year, organized the Twin City Draft Information Center along with his brother Doug, Don Olson, and Sandy Wilkenson. Dave Pence, Dan Meyer, and Don Holland and other young men and women soon joined them.

The first national draft-card burning took place in April of 1967. Resisters in many cities, including Minneapolis, began planning for a draft-card return in Minneapolis that took place on October 16, 1967. It was this public card return and resulting pictures and reports that lead to Gutknecht and others being declared "delinquent" and subsequently ordered to report for induction. After refusing induction, they faced indictment, arrest, and trial. The United States Supreme Court reversed Gutknecht's conviction for this offense. The Supreme Court ruled in Gutknecht's case that the process of declaring a registrant "delinquent" and ordering that person's immediate induction was not authorized by law and, thus, was illegal. The ruling was a major blow to the selective service and resulted in a significant disruption of their enforcement process.

Francis Shor

On January 15, 1968, Francis Shor appeared at the Minneapolis military induction center with his wife and about sixty supporters. He was described by the Minneapolis news as "lanky," "shaved, clean cut and not discourteous." The reporter continued his description of the event as follows:

> He stood quietly at one end of a long hall, appearing out of place, even among the other long-haired, hero-jacketed inductees.

> Shor wore a hero-jacket with the letter "P" representing awards won in three years as a varsity letterman in track and country at the University of Pittsburgh.

> Shor talked with the other inductees, telling them they had rights and that he intended to refuse induction. He described his conduct as follows: "It took me some time to communicate with the other guys because I wasn't sure if I should infringe upon their privacy."

4

Shor, unlike Pence and Gutknecht, was not a native Minnesotan. He was born and raised in the Pittsburgh area where his family still resided. His father owned a small store and was a part-time musician who, in 1999, led a band called the "Swinging Seniors." Shor thought his family was always "more progressive" than that of his high school contemporaries. In 1963, after high school, he attended the University of Pittsburgh and became part of the local antiwar and resistance movement in 1966. He graduated in 1967 with a B.A. in political science, worked on an antiwar education project called Vietnam Summer 1967, volunteered with American Friends Service Committee as a draft counselor in suburban Chicago and became very committed to massive draft-card turn-ins as a way to stop the war.

Fran arrived in Minneapolis in the fall of 1967 having been admitted to graduate school at the University of Minnesota in American Studies. His antiwar, antidraft activities increased. After taking part in

January 15, 1968. Fran Shor in his University of Pittsburgh "P" jacket greeting friends after he refused induction. (Photo by Gillis, from the *Minneapolis Star-Tribune* News Negative Collection. Courtesy of the Minnesota Historical Society)

the October 1967 demonstration at the Pentagon, Shor came back and participated in a sit-in at the university president's office over the issue of Dow Chemical recruiters on campus. Fran became one of the unofficial leaders of antiwar activities on the University of Minnesota campus.

Shortly after he began living with his wife, Peggy, he received his induction order and knew he would publicly refuse induction. They were certain that he would be arrested and that he would go to prison, so the Sunday before he refused induction, he and Peggy were married in a quickly arranged ceremony at the Unitarian Church before his friends in the resistance and antiwar movement.

In January 1968 Shor, Pence, and Gutknecht separately refused induction. Each refusal was accompanied by media coverage and a rally by supporters at the induction center.

On March 2, 1968, the *Minneapolis Tribune* ran a story by staff writer, Bob Lundegaard, who was to write often about the Vietnam War. The story reported their indictments and featured pictures of Pence and Gutknecht over the legend: "Had 'Hershey's' priorities." Selective Service Director Lewis B. Hershey had issued a directive ordering the reclassification to 1A and immediate induction of anyone who turned in his draft card. In addition, he wrote letters to the local boards urging them to move immediately against those who become "delinquent."

In light of the flood of Selective Service indictments that were to follow, it seems strange for so much media attention to be devoted to just three or four draft resisters. But few people had actually been called for induction in Minnesota prior to that and fewer still had openly resisted the draft.

The Bondhus Family

The first reported antidraft case in Minnesota involved a young man from rural Minnesota whose actions were unrelated to the growing resistance movement in the state. Barry Bondhus lived with his parents and nine brothers on a family farm near Big Lake, Minnesota. They were apparently a close-knit family committed to and deeply motivated by iconoclastic fundamentalist religious views. When ordered to report for his pre-induction physical, he refused to cooperate. Later, on February 23, 1966, when his induction order appeared imminent, he dumped two buckets of human waste into several draft-board file cabinets at Elk River, Minnesota. Apparently Bondhus, and his nine brothers gathered up their personal manure after discussions with their parents at the farm. Resisters in the Twin Cities called it, "The movement that started a movement."

Douglas Hall, Minneapolis attorney, served as Bondhus' attorney. He created and led the Minneapolis Legal Rights Center for over three decades. An icon of Minnesota attorneys devoted to the cause of the disenfranchised in every aspect of society, Hall also served as attorney for Pence and other early resisters.

Fran Galt

Fran Galt was probably the first pacifist arrested in Minnesota during the Vietnam era. Galt was born in North Dakota in 1946 and graduated from Dickenson High School in western North Dakota in 1964. His father had a parish as a Methodist minister at the time. When Fran turned eighteen, his parents were living in Audubon, Iowa, and Selective Service insisted that he use their address. Galt said he mailed his draft card back to the board a few weeks after he received it. He referred to his position as "non-cooperation." "It never occurred to me that I would ever go into the military."

Galt was raised as a pacifist. His parents were both missionaries in China on December 7, 1941. They were interned by the Japanese and spent several years in internment camps. During the war, they were exchanged with American prisoners of war, and his father was ordered into service with the U.S. Army. His father refused and was sentenced to five years in prison. He did time with well-known war resisters Bayard Rustin and Dave Dellinger.

Galt grew up with that legacy and with the literature of the Fellowship for Reconciliation (FOR) and the War Resisters League.

He and his brother and friends had gone to Mississippi in 1964 to work on the civil rights voter registration campaign. His father moved to a parish in rural Alabama and remained there.

Galt ignored a letter ordering him to take a physical as well as a notice of a registered letter which he assumed, correctly, was an order to report for induction. He was arrested in St. Paul on a warrant from Iowa. He pled guilty before Judge Stephenson in Des Moines and was sentenced to four years in prison.

Opposition to the War Grows

The angry actions of the Bondhus family, Galt's "non-cooperation" in 1966, and the "resistance" of Pence, Gutknecht, and Shor in 1967 occurred as the war in Vietnam increasingly became an American war. Opposition to American involvement increased in Minnesota.

In March of 1966, the Minnesota Committee to End the War in Vietnam observed an International Day of Protest. Hundreds gathered at the First Unitarian Society in Minneapolis, hundreds more paraded on Saturday, the 26th, through downtown Minneapolis. Traffic backed up as the antiwar demonstration stretched for three blocks. Similar demonstrations were held in other cities.

March 26, 1966. Speakers addressed the marchers in front of the Minneapolis Induction Center. (Photo by Miller from the *Minneapolis Star-Tribune* News Negative Collection. Courtesy of the Minnesota Historical Society)

Sixty-five prominent University of Minnesota professors, artists, and doctors joined others in signing a petition against the war, which appeared in the June 7, 1966, *New York Times*. Another significant march and rally was held on August 6, 1966. The *Minneapolis Tribune* of August 7, 1967, described the march as follows:

> The marchers ranged from professors to hairy peacenik types. There were babes in arms, strollers, and wagons, and, in one case, a car seat slung over the mother's back. Marching briskly with the group was Douglas Campbell, artistic director of the Minnesota Theatre Company, who was wearing bermuda shorts, and controversial Professor Mulford Q. Sibley was wearing his familiar red tie. The banners ranged from the frantic to the frivolous. Among them: "Why Die for Goldwater Policy," "Sanity, Not Body Counts," "Stop the Escalator, I Want to Get Off," "Reconciliation Not Revenge," "Policeman of the World—By What Right?" Following the march the rally resumed at May Auditorium at the University of Minnesota to a capacity crowd."

9

Antiwar activities grew throughout the nation during 1967. In Minnesota, these activities began to take a different and much broader form when high school discussion groups often focused on the draft problems. I first met Dave Gutknecht when he was organizing draft information activity in our local high school, and my oldest son, along with other neighborhood young people, began holding meetings in our basement. Minnesota DFL members met and organized a group known as "Minnesota Dissenting Democrats" aimed at opposing the administration's policy in Vietnam and raising money and support for peace candidates. Similar groups were organizing throughout the country.

The first person to go to prison in Minnesota who was part of an organized opposition to the war was Robert Gilliam, a twenty-two-year-old pacifist who worked for the *Catholic Worker* magazine in New York City before his arrest in July 1967. Gilliam was a theology student who had graduated from St. Mary's College and applied for conscientious-objector status. In September 1966, he returned his draft card to his selective service board and, thereafter, refused to cooperate with the board. His sentencing was preceded by a "peace vigil" with Gilliam, clergymen, and pacifists at the Minneapolis headquarters of the Vietnam Summer Project. Gilliam plead guilty to refusing to accept induction and appeared at sentencing without counsel. There were about eighty supporters in the courtroom. Gilliam spoke clearly to his rejection of "the demands of the state." "It wants our approval of institutionalized violence. . . ." He appeared before by U.S. Federal Judge Earl Larson, who sentenced Gilliam to two years in prison and stated that because Gilliam had violated the law, "I feel I do have to impose a penalty, but I am sure you will use your time well."

In early February, 1968, a twenty-two-year-old student attending Oxford on a Rhodes Scholarship mailed his draft card in to his draft board in Redwood Falls, Minnesota, and was declared delinquent and classified 1A.

In April 1968, just days before the assassination of Martin Luther King, nine draft cards were turned in to the United States attorney by Don Olson and others during a rally at the Minneapolis Federal Building as part of the Third National Day of Resistance.

By the time Pence and Gutknecht were indicted on March 1, 1968, the Twin Cities Draft Information Center (TCDIC) was running full speed. Gutknecht and two others worked there full time along with many volunteers The organization was at the center of the outreach to high-school and draft-age men seeking to organize opposition to the draft and offered help to anyone seeking alternatives to the draft or advice coping with draft-related problems. During 1968 and 1969 TCDIC counseled 100 young men per week.

Gutknecht was arrested on March 4, 1968, while staffing an information booth on alternatives to the draft at the Coffman (student) Union on the University of Minnesota campus. Pence was arrested the same day at his home.

A large antiwar rally took place in Minneapolis on July 10, 1968. On August 7, 1968, over 500 people gathered at the Universalist Church in Minneapolis, which became the focal point for much of the draft resistance and religious-focused antiwar activity. The main speaker was Father Phillip Salem, a Catholic priest who earlier that year had sent letters to 800 high school seniors in Duluth urging them to resist the draft and refuse service in Vietnam. Seventeen men, including ten clergymen turned in their selective service cards, and large groups of clergymen, nuns, and lay persons signed a letter urging draft-age men to resist the draft.

Dan Holland - George Crocker

Uncle Sam wore suede boots and Professor Mulford Sibley showed up in sandals as [sixty] antiwar protestors turned out Monday to cheer Dan Holland, Caledonia, Minnesota, for refusing to submit to induction into the armed forces.

That was the lead sentence of the *Minneapolis Tribune* article on September 24, 1968, describing the events at Holland's processing.

11

The article featured a picture of Holland and the rally, featuring "Uncle Sam."

Uncle Sam turned out to be George Crocker. Crocker, one of the best-known and most recognized pacifist antiwar activists, had refused induction in February 1968. His family were Quakers. His father had gone to prison during World War II for refusing induction. George worked at the Twin Cities Draft Information Center almost from the time it was organized. Early on the morning of October 15, 1968, Crocker gathered with others at the induction center in support of Sydney Walter, thirty-three, artistic director of the Firehouse Theater in Minneapolis, who refused induction. Walter had been ordered for induction for returning his draft card to his local board.

September 25, 1968, George Crocker in Uncle Sam suit and Mulford Sibley in front of the Minneapolis Induction Center. (Photo by Zerby from the *Minneapolis Star-Tribune* News Negative Collection. Courtesy of the Minnesota Historical Society)

About 150 persons watched antiwar skits and sang resistance songs. Crocker participated in his "Uncle Sam" suit in one of the skits. After Walter emerged from the center, it appeared that Crocker was about to be arrested. He and his friends drove to the Universalist Church, and, with the approval of the minister, the first Minnesota antiwar, antidraft church "sanctuary" was declared. A black-and-white resistance flag hung over the main door of the church.

It lasted less than one day. The F.B.I. came into the church and

March 18, 1969, Dan Holland (in plaid shirt facing camera on far side of circle) and other anti-war protesters held peace "celebration" at the Minneapolis Induction Center. (Photo by Heine, from the *Minneapolis Star-Tribune* Collection, Courtesy of the Minnestoa Historical Society)

pushed their way through the crowd. Crocker, who earlier that day had stressed to the crowd that he wanted no violence, asked the group to stop resisting: "We have made our point, friends," he said.

George Crocker would later be sentenced to four years in prison, reduced on a motion to three years, the longest executed sentence for refusing induction during the Vietnam era in Minnesota. Pence (three years), Gutknecht (four years), and John Crocker (three years) were all cases reversed by the Court of Appeals.

A memorable ceremony took place on November 14, 1968, at the First Unitarian Society with more than 1,200 participants. Dr. Spock was the featured speaker. Thirty-nine men including several veterans turned in their cards; two eighteen-year olds announced their non-registration. Among the new resisters were John Crocker, eighteen, who refused to register, and Herbert Crocker, twenty-one, who turned in his student deferment. Both were brothers of George Crocker.

In November 1968, a large march into downtown Minneapolis featured a "Happy Resistance Day Costume" parade. Another event was an announced plan to burn a dog by antiwar protesters in St. Cloud, Minnesota, which caused the governor of Minnesota to make sure St. Cloud authorities prevented this "senseless killing." It soon became obvious that no one intended to burn a dog—only to make the point that so many were concerned by that threat, but none did anything to stop the napalming of people in Vietnam.

By early 1969, the Twin Cities Draft Information Center began organizing in public schools to teach students and adults about the draft. The Minneapolis School Board threatened to cancel the class and evict the participants, but public pressure persuaded the board to withdraw the threat.

In March 1969, seventeen-year-old Scott Alarik, a student at West High in Minneapolis led a group of sixteen young men who publicly declared they would not register for the draft. Dave Gutknecht and others put out an anti-registration booklet titled, "Check Out the Odds: If Your Name's Not in the Lottery Your Number Can't Come Up." Alarik distributed it at West High. The West High principal wrote a letter to Alarik's local board that resulted in Alarik's indictment shortly after his graduation.

Most of the persons arrested and indicted made little impact in the media. The press took notice of the arrest or indictment of persons of some personal notoriety such as an army officer's daughter opposing the draft or a Rhodes scholar or the president of the student council.

While most arrests were without incident, some were highly staged events. After twenty-year-old Daniel Holland was indicted, he was among thirty activists who entered the induction center with cake and apple cider along with a man dressed as a specter of death that chanted the name of men killed in Vietnam. They had expected Holland to be arrested. Instead the group was evicted.

Opposition Grows

On October 15, 1969, Minnesota participated in a nation-wide rally/religious requiem for peace called Vietnam Moratorium Day. At the University of Minnesota, about half of the 40,000 students attended antiwar lectures, "teach-ins," and "truth-outs." A morning rally drew over 10,000 people to downtown Minneapolis. At 9:00 A.M. people filled the large plaza in front of Coffman Memorial Union on the University of Minnesota campus. They spilled over onto the footbridges that spanned Washington Avenue.

Later, the crowd made a one-mile march to the armed forces induction center. They filled almost every foot of space between the Federal Building and the Milwaukee Railroad station across the street and between Washington Avenue and Second Street South.

A small group broke off around 2:00 and moved to the Nicollet Mall intent upon disruption and confrontation with the police. Bill Tilton, vice president of the Minnesota Student Association and one of the organizers of the Vietnam Moratorium activities in the Twin Cities went to work.

> Up and down the mall he roamed, pleading: "Let's work for peace . . . break it up. You're not doing any good for peace that way. This is what the Stenvig (Minneapolis Mayor Charles Stenvig—former police officer) wants you to do."

> "Please, we've served our purpose downtown.
> We can do no more good right here."

This is the same William Tilton who, less than a year later, was arrested in Alexandria, Minnesota, at midnight inside a draft board intent on destroying draft records. He was convicted and sent to prison.

Augsburg and Hamline classes were suspended on Vietnam Moratorium Day and a wide variety of antiwar activities were held. Speakers at Hamline University included Representative Donald Fraser and Minnesota Supreme Court Justice James Otis. Macalester College and St. Thomas College and many Twin City high schools had requiems, workshops, symposiums, speakers, and discussion groups.

Macalester students organized teams to visit local government officials, business executives, and religious leaders. The most exciting program was the night rally at the field house on the campus of Macalester College. Senator Walter Mondale and Julian Bond spoke. Bond had been elected to the Georgian House of Representatives in 1965. The Georgia house excluded him because of his statements criticizing the war in Vietnam and the operation of the Selective Service System. He sought judicial relief, which was denied by a local court panel. The United States Supreme Court unanimously reversed that decision and entered an order requiring him to be seated.

Bond had been director of the Student Nonviolent Coordinating Committee, a civil rights organization, and may have disappointed some in the audience by his soft-spoken style. But he did not disappoint those who listened carefully to his well-crafted and wide-ranging attacks on his United States involvement in the war and the selective service system.

Walter Mondale clearly stole the day as he surprised the audience, and indeed the whole country, by appearing to break clearly from continued support of the war.

In 1964 President Johnson had obtained approval from Congress to continue and expand the Vietnam War based upon an alleged unprovoked attack by North Vietnam on United States Navy ships in the Gulf of Tonkin. Later this claim was widely recognized as a fraud, in that no such attack took place, and in 1969 Senator Fulbright and others called for revoking the resolution. Mondale joined Fulbright to support revocation of the Gulf of Tonkin resolution and called for an end to the war.

The front page of the *St. Paul Pioneer Press* for October 16, 1969, was filled with Moratorium Day news. The largest headline was: "Thousands Take Part in Viet Moratorium," with the subhead "War Opponents, Backers Take to the Streets." That story featured the candlelight march on the White House, and the widow of Martin Luther King pleading with the president to "bring the boys home, and bring them home now." On the opposite side of the front page just under the masthead was the story from Macalester College in St. Paul; the headline "Mondale: Pull Out the Troops." After describing the cheering crowd the story continued:

> Mondale said the United States must "Openly and frankly say: we were in error and pull out the troops.
> I now admit my mistake, and I think the government of the United States should do the same."

Elsewhere on the front page, the following stories appeared following the underlined headlines:

"Marine Base Shelled by Reds." The story described the shelling of the artillery base in Vietnam manned by U.S. Marines being withdrawn from an outpost just south of the demilitarized zone. It also describes troops who "wore black armbands in support of Moratorium Day."

"Congressional Leaders Slap Hanoi Letter." The premier of North Vietnam wrote a letter supporting the nationwide moratorium. House and Senate leaders criticized the letter but not the call for a moratorium.

"Laird Sees Viet Pull-out in Year or Two." Defense

March 16, 1971. Vietnam Veterans for Peace rally at Minnesota State Capitol. (From the *Minneapolis Star-Tribune* News Negative Collection. Courtesy of the Minnesota Historical Society)

Secretary Melvin Laird stated in a recorded interview that "there is no question" but that the United States can withdraw all of its combat troops from Vietnam within a year or two.

On January 19, 1970, a Minnesota Grand Jury handed down a record forty-two indictments alleging violation of selective service laws, mostly the failure to report for induction. The forty-two indictments overshadowed the thirty-one non-selective service cases handed down by that Grand Jury report. The previous report for selective service indictments was in October of 1969, less than three months previously when the Grand Jury indicted thirty-two.

On May 2, 1970, President Nixon ordered the United States to invade Cambodia. A national student strike resulted. Ohio National Guardsman killed four students participating in the strike on the Kent State campus. On May 9, 1970, in response to the Cambodian invasion and the killing of the Kent State students possibly the largest gathering

Peace marchers approached the State Capitol nearing the end of a trek from the University of Minnesota. (Photo by Kobersteen from the *Minneapolis Star-Tribune* News Negative Collection. Courtesy of the Minnesota Historical Society)

of its kind took place in the Twin Cities. An antiwar march began at noon at the Minneapolis campus of the University of Minnesota, and the last of the crowd arrived at the State Capital four hours later. I was one of the captains of the 500 "marshals" consisting mainly of lawyers, legal workers, and clergymen. We estimated the gathering at the Capital as 100,000 strong. Capital police gave the figure of 50,000, while St. Paul police said 20,000 to 25,000. It was a major demonstration of antiwar sentiment that drew Republican Governor Harold LeVander out of his office with a request to speak and greet the crowd, which he did.

An editorial in the Minneapolis paper described the march as "historic," ". . . too large to be ignored," "20,000 to 50,000 marchers." More important, the editorial made reference to a recent Minnesota poll showing eighty percent of Minnesotans wanted to withdraw from

May 10, 1972, 5,000 March through Mankato calling for the end of the war. Part of the crowd during the three days of protests on college campuses and cities throughout the state. (Photo by Robertson; from the *Minneapolis Star-Tribune* News Negative Collection; courtesy of the Minnesota Historical Society)

Vietnam and eighty-six percent felt that the administration had made no progress in ending the war.

As antiwar sentiment grew, stories began to appear concerning activities totally unrelated to the organized student- and clergy-led movement. Ninety employees of Pillsbury met and founded an anti-Vietnam War group. Newly elected D.F.L. Governor Wendel Anderson and Attorney General Warren Spannus, along with Senate D.F.L. Majority Leader Nicholas Coleman came out in support of bills to require the attorney general to file suit declaring the war illegal. The St. Cloud and Minneapolis city councils passed antiwar resolutions, as did the cities of Fargo and Moorhead.

In January 1971, Daniel Ellsberg delivered a report on the origin and conduct on the war in Vietnam to the *New York Times* for publication. The report, dubbed the "Pentagon Papers" began the focus of a United States Supreme Court decision. At the same time, the United States government attempted to prevent its publication.

May 11, 1972. College students and clergy rally at the St. Paul Federal Building. (Photo by Radniecki, from the *Minneapolis Star-Tribune* News Negative Collection; courtesy of the Minnesota Historical Society)

In late June 1971, the Supreme Court struck down the efforts to prevent publication.

In September 1971, a federal grand jury in Minnesota indicted 132 men for violation of the Selective Service Act. Forty-eight were indicted for all other non-draft related criminal offenses. In October, Lieutenant Governor Rudy Perpich led many other Minnesota elected officials in support of a Vietnam War Moratorium Day. The Minneapolis Federation of Teachers encouraged its 12,000 members to devote a portion of their class time to a discussion of the Vietnam War. In November forty-eight more people were indicted for selective service act violations. In addition, the U.S. Attorney began arresting young men who refused induction without indictments.

On July 28, 1999, I interviewed Thor Anderson, then a Hennepin County district court judge. From 1968 through 1973, he was primarily responsible for the handling of Selective Service cases and tried many. Anderson said, "There was a period near the end of the draft when I (and others) from the U.S. Attorney's office showed up at the induction center, and when young men refused induction, we would fill out a criminal complaint and serve it on them immediately in an effort to get them to change their mind and accept induction." Anderson explained that he wanted to dispel the notion that it would be a long time before their case came up or perhaps they would never be charged. He advised the young men who refused induction, and to whom he gave complaints, that they would go to court immediately, and, even if released on bail, their cases would go the Grand Jury for indictment within the month.

In fiscal year 1972 (July 1, 1971 through June 30, 1972) in Minnesota, 726 criminal cases were commenced of which 387 (fifty-three percent) were selective service cases. On June 30, 1972, 390 criminal cases were pending. Two-hundred-thirty-five (sixty percent) were selective service cases.

It is likely that Minnesota had one of the highest draft prosecution rates in the country.

21

Chapter Two

The Draft

Colonial America had a clear distrust of the national military conscription that became common throughout Europe following
the French Revolution.

Even during the Revolutionary War, there was no general conscription, although the colonies had a variety of programs relating to service in the colonial militia some of which could be described as relating
roughly to a conscription program. There was a national conscription
during the Civil War, but it was essentially used as an inducement to
raise bounties for volunteers. That is, those who had money escaped
the army by paying others to volunteer. The opposition to the Civil War
draft led to the biggest riots in United States history, at least until the
1960s, one hundred years later.

From the late 1800s up to the United States entry into World
War I in 1917, millions of people immigrated to the United States not
only to seek a better life and flee starvation and oppression but also to
avoid compulsory service in the armies of Europe, Scandinavia, and
Tsarist Russia. Indeed, my family history and the history of almost every
person I knew as a young man was heavily seasoned with stories of parents, uncles, grandparents, and others who came to this country in part

to escape compulsory service in an army and often as an immediate response to threatened conscription.

World War I was fought by state units and augmented by a general draft. The draft was managed by local boards that were given substantial power to grant deferments based upon the needs of industry and farming. The World War I draft was primarily a method of controlling general manpower needs. Although selection into the armed forces was through a national lottery, a secondary purpose of the system seemed to be to punish those who opposed United States entry into the war. The World War I experience led to the use of the local board system for the more general draft, which was adopted in 1940 as the United States was being inevitably drawn into World War II. The local board system has prevailed ever since.

Since 1940, America has had a compulsory service system every year (except 1947), and it was an established part of American life. Yet, by 1993 it was defunct. And it has been dead ever since.

The major problem through most of the years between World War II and the war in Vietnam was an overabundance of eligible young men. During World War II, the oldest available were drafted first. President Kennedy sought to relieve the problem of overabundance of eligible young men by reversing the process and placing all married men at the bottom of the sequence and granting automatic deferment to students. It was during this period that programs were promoted to use the army to promote social rehabilitation and the war on poverty.

Things changed in 1964, as Vietnam became a conflagration that engulfed the nation. At that time, the draft laws were governed by the Universal Military and Training Act of 1951. Under that law, all men had to register for the draft at the age of eighteen and remained liable for service from age eighteen and one half and to age twenty-six. After registration, a person was classified in the order of his potential for induction. The tour of draftee's active service was twenty-four months. New authority to induct had to be obtained every four years. One of the main reasons for the acceptance of the draft in the pre-Vietnam era was the simple fact that few young men were drafted. Deferments flowed from the draft in ever increasing numbers, and the prime draft age group of nineteen- to twenty-five-year olds grew from eight million in 1958 to twelve million in 1964.

As protest against the Vietnam War and the draft escalated, the local boards, under the direction of General Hershey, followed a practice of ordering the immediate induction of anyone who failed to do anything required of him by the law or draft-board rules. That included everything from not registering for the draft to failing to keep the board informed of a current address. The most common reason for declaring a registrant "delinquent" and ordering him inducted was mailing a draft card back to a local board, which violated the rule that the card must be kept in one's possession.

In the fall of 1965, a group of students and faculty members at the University of Michigan sat in at their local board in Ann Arbor, Michigan. The Michigan State director called General Hershey and they agreed that the proper response was to remove deferments from any protesters and order their induction. In February 1966, then Assistant Attorney General Fred Vinson announced that the draft "shall not be used to end dissent." General Hershey replied, in effect, that he was in charge of administrating the selective service "and there's no question about who makes the law." The president of Yale, Kingston Brewster, told the 1966 graduating class that the draft had made a mockery of service to the nation.

General Lewis B. Hershey was instrumental in the planning of the 1940 draft laws, and after those draft laws were enacted, General Hershey (then a lieutenant-colonel) wrote the regulations and became the assistant director under the nominal civilian head. Shortly after World War II ended, he became director of the Selective Service system and remained in that position until 1970, when President Nixon forced the seventy-five-year-old general to resign in an effort to deflect the growing antidraft sentiment in the country.

Almost three years earlier, President Johnson's response to opposition to the draft laws was to appoint a commission under the direction of Burke Marshall, former head of the Civil Rights Division in the United States Department of Justice. The 1967 report, most often referred to as the Marshall Commission report, was entitled: *Pursuit of Equity: Who Should Serve When Not All Serve.* The commission proposed many changes and reforms, including a total overhaul of the local board system as unrepresentative of age, race, economic status, and just about every other imaginable parameter. It also proposed the immediate institution of a random selection system to replace the antiquated order of call regulations. Congress rejected almost all proposals.

In lieu of reform, Congress provided a blanket deferment for all undergraduates until graduation and provided for the drafting of the youngest men first. The latter was President Johnson's proposal. The new law, designated as "The Military Selective Service Act of 1967," did order the development of a lottery system but required specific congressional approval before the system could go into effect. The revised law also made conscientious objector rules easier to administer and more consistent with court decisions and required a report to Congress on the disposition of every draft-violation case. The only hint of reform in the bill was that women became eligible for local board membership.

The results of the reform effort increased opposition to the draft. Foremost was the call to increase prosecution of the draft law violators. Secondary to this was the decision to eliminate almost all postgraduate deferments. In fact, the Department of Justice was prosecuting violators with unprecedented vigor, and prosecutions continued to increase, reaching 4,000 in 1969. About 25,000 men were indicted out of over 200,000 identified violators during the Vietnam War but this percentage was consistent with charges and indictments for all crimes in the American judicial system.

The director of the Selective Service regularly delivers and publishes reports to the United States Congress. Since 1967 these reports have been semi-annual. The report for the fiscal year ending July 1, 1967, began with "The Year's Highlights."

*A critical year—a combination of events and circum-
stances made fiscal 1967 a busy and critical one for the Selective
Service System. The tempo of the war in Vietnam increased,
some small groups demonstrated against the Nation's participation there, accompanied by protest against the operation of
Selective Service—even demands for its abolition.*

Nonetheless, the report pointed out that over one-third of the
nation's male citizens were Selective Service registrants. About 300,000
persons were drafted in fiscal 1967, and over 459,000 were enlisted in
the armed forces along with over 95,000 enlistments in the National
Guard and Reserves. Thus, close to 850,000 American men were
brought into service in that twelve-month period directly or indirectly as
a result of the war in Vietnam and the draft.

Following a detailed discussion of the various studies and recommendations and listing the changes in the newly enacted Military
Selective Service Act of 1967, the report moved to a new section entitled "The Year in Review" and once again began a discussion of criti-
cisms of the draft and its response. It basically defended the local board
system as one that prevented the alleged injustice and inequity that it
claimed would result from ignoring variations in circumstance among
individuals and localities. While clearly the local board system had little
to recommend it, attacks on the draft were based primarily upon the
draft itself and its use to support the war in Vietnam. The best that could
be said for the system was that it apparently was preferred by Congress
to the suggestions of the study commission and appeared to place the
Congress on the side of General Hershey and not the president.

The December 31, 1967, report again emphasized the directive
from General Hershey to the local boards to place men who became
delinquent in the first call for induction. The report saw this as needed
because of the increase in illegal activities at local boards, induction cen-
ters, and college campuses. Indeed most of the summary for that period was an effort to justify that process and appeared quite testy about
criticism.

The next reporting period, June 20, 1968, acknowledged that, for the first time in twenty years, the manpower requests were not met; that criticism of the draft or protest against it played a part in that problem, that activities were directed at "legalistic tests of enforcement" in the court. In the section on law enforcement, it claimed its treatment of Selective Service violators was *"controversial and somewhat misunderstood,"* but it touted the delinquency punitive induction process while acknowledging that it was being "tested in the country." It was a remarkable document. Its tone was defiant and self-righteous as the enforcer of the obligation that all "obey the laws from which his freedom flows." To accomplish this objective the *"system . . . will use . . . the exclusive administrative powers of the local board to reclassify, declare delinquent, and forward for accelerated induction delinquent registrants."* This remarkable document suggested that the director of the Selective Service system had *"ultimate responsibility to bring democratic principles into perspective . . . if national unity and cohesiveness is to be restored and national survival assured."*

In February 1970, General Hershey resigned as director of the Selective Service. Curtis Tarr replaced him, and the semi-annual reports to Congress took on a new, "folksy" tone and a new look with drawings and cartoons. In his first report for the period ending June 30, 1970, he described in detail the destruction of draft records at state headquarters in Washington, Delaware, and in Rhode Island. He described them as being "hit."

In the December 1970 report, he described his visit to Vietnam to meet with and talk to young servicemen about the draft. He "slithered" through mud and "ducked" into a tin shack. His conclusion: random selection was the way to go.

Director Tarr noted in his report that in June of 1970, 14,440 registrants filed applications for conscientious objector status.

By 1972, 130.72 legal conscientious objector classifications would be granted for every 100 persons inducted. That is 1.3 persons granted C.O. classification for every person inducted. The rate during World War II was 0.5 per hundred.

In the June 30, 1971, report, Director Tarr saw the most critical problem facing the system as "enforcement of the laws" but "rejoice[d]" in the Supreme Court decision reversing the conviction of Muhammad Ali as we must "each time our country pronounces the requirements of justice, even though opinions differ."

In the concluding narrative of the report, Director Tarr told the tale of Pocahontas saving the life of John Smith, marrying John Rolfe and sending a warrior off to England to meet the English with instructions to count the number of Englishmen he encountered by cutting notches on a wooden stick. Unable to accomplish the assignment, he allegedly reported: *"Count all the stars in the sky, all the leaves on the trees, all the grains of sand on the seashore: all of these, even more, are the people of England."*

The only point I can deduce is that the warrior was a poor statistician but capable of dramatic prose. The story is infantile, false and racist.

The December 31, 1971, report of Director Tarr to Congress detailed efforts to beef up prosecutors at every level; the conclusion told the tale of a conscientious objector doing alternative service with the California division of forestry. In short, he saved a giant sequoia tree. It's there for every Congressman (and citizen) to read as proof of how well our system works.

Chapter Three

Judging

T he acts of the judges in deciding selective service cases during the Vietnam War are clear. Judge Devitt found most of the defendants who appeared before him guilty and sentenced them more harshly than his colleagues. I developed an "equivalency scale" in order to compare the sentences of the judges in this study. The scale is described in the appendix. By using the scale, I produced a score for each judge, i.e. an "E-score." Judge Devitt's E-score was 8.44. Judge Larson found defendants guilty at about the same rate as Judge Devitt but sentenced them more lightly (E-score 5.57). Judge Neville found significantly fewer defendants guilty than either Judges Devitt or Larson, but sentenced almost as harshly as Judge Devitt (E-score 8.03) and Judge Lord found the fewest defendants guilty and handed out the lightest sentences (E-score 3.03).

It is more difficult to determine why the judges acted as they did. Courts are required to set out the basis for their decisions, but they are not required to write opinions or memoranda explaining their decisions. The judges differ greatly in the frequency with which they wrote memoranda or opinions. In addition these memoranda vary from complex well-supported analyses to brief conclusions.

Unlike most appellate court opinions that are officially published and widely circulated, district court opinions, while public, are not generally published or circulated. They are, of course, available to be examined as part of the court file. In addition a federal judge may send a copy of his memorandum-opinion to be published in the "Federal Supplement." That publication is readily available to the bench and bar. It is apparent that the judges differ greatly in their practice with respect to sending their opinions to the Federal Supplement for publication.

Thus the number of memoranda-decisions published and unpublished for each of the judges reflects some judgment on the part of each judge of the significance of their decision for the bench and bar. It may also reflect in some cases upon the judge's ego.

I found the following memoranda for each judge:

JUDGE	TOTAL NUMBER OF MEMOS	TOTAL NUMBER PUBLISHED
Judge Devitt	24	12
Judge Lord	12	2
Judge Neville	55	27
Judge Larson	33	7

Chapter Four

Judge Miles Lord

"I probably did that."
    Judge Lord in acknowledging that in 1968 at their first bail hearing, he suggested that Pence and Gutknecht should get a taste of jail and announcing in 1972 that draft-case defendants could plead guilty and go home.

On March 5, 1968, Pence and Gutknecht were brought before Judge Miles Lord for arraignment. Bail had been set at $3,000 for each defendant. Doug Hall made a motion to reduce Pence's bail. Judge Lord reduced bail for Pence to $1,500 but refused to release him to his attorney. The paper quotes Judge Lord as stating that they should "get a taste of prison" now. They quote the judge further as follows:

> After they have a few days in jail and get an idea of what the regimentation is there, and how the freedoms for which they fight and protest will be deprived of them for two years, they might more seriously consider the course they are taking.

In lowering Pence's bail, Lord said he hoped that "if he has friends and relatives they won't make bail for him." On March 16, 1968, the *Minneapolis Tribune* published two letters to the editor highly critical of Judge Lord. One letter wrote in part:

> I assume you have misquoted Judge Lord. If so, you owe him a public apology. Certainly he would not threaten these young men with imprisonment to deter them from exercising their legal rights, imprison them as criminals before they are tried, or prejudge their guilt or innocence. He certainly would not use the prestige of his high judicial office to dissuade their friends and relatives from making bail for these young men after he has judicially found they are entitled to it.

A second letter was briefer. It read simply:

> It would appear that a judge who is so certain that these men will be convicted that he recommends a preview of jail for them should not be trying this case.

An editor's note followed the first letter—". . . Judge Lord was quoted accurately."

On March 22, 1968, Judge Lord removed himself from the case.

In the ensuing Vietnam era, Judge Lord would adjudicate eighty-four selective service cases. Forty-seven of those cases were tried to the court without a jury. He found only eighteen guilty, which is an acquittal rate of sixty-two percent. Adding to those eighteen he found guilty, those who were found guilty by a jury (six) and those who pled guilty before him (thirty) he was called to sentence fifty-four young men for selective service violations. He sent only seven to prison for an average of six months each.

The details concerning Judge Lord and the other District Court judges' convictions and sentencing appear in the attached appendix.

In 1972, at a time when Selective Service indictments constituted over fifty percent of the federal criminal cases in Minnesota, Judge Lord announced from the bench at arraignments that any defendant present who was charged with a Selective Service violation and wanted his case disposed of forthwith should step forward. He amplified his statement by indicating that he would accept a guilty plea, put the defendant on probation, and the defendant could go on his way.

Judge Miles Lord was born on a farm in Crow Wing County, Minnesota, on Minnesota's Iron Range. He was one of nine children. His brothers founded the Steelworkers Union in Minnesota. His father was a disabled miner who supported his family by operating a taxi and delivery service with a team of horses. Lord graduated high school and junior college at Crosby-Ironton and then went to the University of Minnesota. In 1948 he graduated from the University of

Judge Miles Lord. (Courtesy of the Minnesota Historical Society)

Minnesota Law School. He practiced law for a few years, made an unsuccessful run for the state legislature, and in 1951 became an assistant U.S. Attorney. Folklore has it, that no one wanted to run for Minnesota Attorney General on the D.F.L. ticket in 1954 against a long-time Republican incumbent. Lord received the uncontested endorsement, won election and began a career as Attorney General, U.S. Attorney (1961), and Federal Judge (1966) that ended thirty-one years later in 1985 when he retired from the bench.

It is commonplace to describe his career as controversial. Certainly this is true. But the details are involved and complex. He knew and understood the tremendous power a federal judge had and used it to the fullest. To those interested in the more widely published battles of his career, see the endnotes. There I have references to his censure in 1954 by the Minnesota Supreme Court for his advice as Attorney General to County Attorneys to ignore a court order; his nine-month battle with Reserve Mining, resulting in a halt to the discharging of taconite tailings into Lake Superior, and his removal from the case by the Eighth Circuit Judicial Court for "gross bias" against Reserve, his rebuke by a panel of the Eighth Circuit for remarks he made to major pharmacy firms for price fixing; his lecture to Dalkon Shield officials for planting "instruments of death, mutilation, and disease in thousands of women" and much more.

I knew Judge Lord as a man who offered to stand up for me when I might have needed his help and as a man who was petty and backbiting when we were on different sides of a political campaign. I knew him as a man who sometimes tried too hard to help a neighbor or friend in trouble and made "Lord-awful" mistakes of judgment for these very reasons. I also knew him as a man who, more than occasionally, made up his mind about a case before the opening statements were completed. He was hard of hearing and vain and turned his wrath on any unsuspecting defendant who did not heed his warning to "speak up!"

In the spring of 1974, I met Arthur Banks. Banks was a large African-American man. Not only was he impressive physically, but he had a large, booming voice. An actor and playwright from the New York stage, his stature and bearing was reminiscent of the famous actor-singer Paul Robeson. Banks had been indicted and convicted in his home state of Indiana for refusing to be inducted into the army. Sentenced to five years in prison, he had spent twenty-seven months in prison—twenty of those months in solitary confinement in the federal prison in Terre Haute, Indiana. After he was transferred to the federal prison in Sandstone, Minnesota, a friend of his made contact with

William Kunstler, who was staying in St. Paul, working on the trial of Dennis Banks and Russell Means arising out of the Wounded Knee events in February through April 1973. As near as we could figure out, the cause of Arthur Banks' prior treatment was that he was black, large, imposing and thus "threatening." We brought a habeas petition before Judge Lord, asking for his release on the grounds of his having been subjected to cruel and inhuman treatment. Lord heard the testimony and turned to the U.S. Attorney for rebuttal. The U.S. Attorney said something about the court having no power over the prison authorities in this situation, that Judge Lord had no jurisdiction simply because Banks happened to be in the state. Before the day was over, Mr. Banks was released on $1,000 bail and returned to his home in New York. A year of multi-state litigation, writs, motions, and appeals followed before Banks was fully freed from the nightmare.

After Judge Lord withdrew from David Pence's case in 1968, he was not faced with another Selective Service case until late spring 1969 when he decided the cases of John W. Hawley and Claude David Schmidt. Both memoranda-decisions were important. Each memorandum included an exhaustive discussion of all relevant authorities on every aspect of the case—along with detailed discussion of the facts and issues.

John Hawley was a twenty-two-year-old college student at the University of Minnesota who was represented by Chester Bruvold. After several student deferments that included a period in law school, he filed a detailed application for conscientious objector status. The record disclosed that his brother was a Methodist minister, that the defendant was active politically and spoke as a member of the War Resisters League. Twenty-six members of the Fridley, Minnesota, Methodist Church from his home community along with a number of university professors and other friends signed letters or petitions on his behalf. His application was denied on the basis that the local board "feels this is not a religious thing but is formed out of a personal moral view." Judge Lord found that the only plausible inference was that the board did not find Mr. Crowley sincere. Earlier that month, the Court of Appeals for the Eighth Circuit had handed down the David Pence decision, reversing Judge Devitt. That case and others held that there must be a factual basis in the record for the draft boards decisions. Thus the issue was whether the record disclosed facts to support the reasons given for denying the C.O. classification. Lord rejected the government argument to the contrary. He relied upon the United States Supreme Court in the 1965 *Seeger* decision that denial of a C.O. claim on the grounds that the petitioner belief is "merely personal" must be understood to mean that merely personal is the sole basis of the petitioner's belief. That is, if the beliefs of the applicant have a religious basis, the fact that he also has non-religious, political, sociological or philosophical views that contribute to his understanding does not mean that the application for C.O. status should be denied. Thus, Judge Lord acquitted Mr. Hawley because there was no "basis in fact" for the decision of the local Selective Service board.

Before the Vietnam draft cases were to run their course, Judge Lord would write five more decisions in which he discussed the need for a factual basis in the record to support the local boards stated reasons for its action. In each of these cases, he acquitted the defendants.

Judge Lord delivered the *Hawley* decision on May 26, 1969. Less than one week later on June 3, 1969, he would find Claude Schmidt guilty. Schmidt also filed a petition for Conscientious Objector status that was denied by the local board. But unlike Hawley, he did not file his application until after the local board had sent out an order for him to report for induction. The Selective Service Regulations required the local board to reopen the file and consider new material after sending out an order to report for induction, only if there had been a change of circumstances over which the applicant had no control. Schmidt's application was detailed and well supported. The board granted Schmidt a courtesy interview in which they discussed his claim at length and permitted him to supplement the record. Schmidt submitted further personal statements and supporting letters and had a second courtesy interview. The board then determined there was no change in circumstance beyond Schmidt's control and refused to reopen his classification. They never decided the case on the merits of the C.O. petition. Larry Leventhal, a 1967 University of Minnesota Law School graduate who was to become one of Minnesota's most successful Selective Service defense attorneys, was Schmidt's attorney. He argued that the board was required to reopen when a conscientious objector claim "crystallized" after the induction order was issued. Judge Lord acknowledged that some courts had adopted such a rule, but that the Eighth Circuit had not specifically decided the question. Furthermore he found that the defendant did not make a showing on that issue which would require the board to reopen. He also rejected the argument, and those cases supporting the argument, that the detailed questioning at the "courtesy" interview was in fact a reopening. Judge Larsen supported that view with considerable force about a month earlier in a case involving James Kerwin.

Judge Lord drew a distinction between a local draft board "considering the merits of the claim" on the one hand and "actually deciding on the merits" on the other.

I find the distinction almost impossible to apply, Judge Lord argued that the board should have the totality of the circumstance before it in making its determination.

> It seems that the relevant facts the board needs—are what the registrant's beliefs are, when and how he acquired them, and why he is asserting them only after receiving his Order to Report for Induction."

The difficulty one has in applying the distinction is underlined by the court itself in acknowledging that the board is not free to determine the merits of the claim but nevertheless foreclose review of the merits "by simply couching it in terms of a refusal to reopen."

Judge Lord felt that the board did not decide on the merits of Schmidt's C.O. petition, thus he convicted Mr. Schmidt. He sentenced him to two years and suspended the sentence on condition he seek and obtain work similar to C.O. type work and do such work for two years.

Before the year was over, Judge Lord would write two additional memoranda in Selective Service cases. Lyle Unnasch, a young dairy farmer from southeastern Minnesota was inexplicably refused his request for a II-C (agricultural) deferment. He was acquitted as was Brian Coyle, a young man from Moorhead, Minnesota, who was an active pacifist and, although raised a Catholic, a member of the Society of Friends. Mr. Coyle, who had been teaching at Moorhead State, College was denied his C.O. claim and ordered to report for induction after he returned his draft card to the board. He failed to report for his physical and was ordered to report for induction as "delinquent." His indictment for refusing to submit to induction was dismissed after the Supreme Court decision in *Gutknecht*. He was re-indicted for refusing to take his physical.

Brian Coyle's indictment for refusing to take a physical was unprecedented. Before *Gutknecht,* no one had been prosecuted for failure to take a physical except as part of an indictment charging failure to accept induction. Judge Lord rejected the government's claim that it could prosecute an interim order even if the 1-A classification on which the interim order was based was not valid. The point was that Coyle was classified 1-A only because he returned his draft card to his board. That was an illegal act by the board. In addition to pointing out that a registrant classified C.O. need not take his physical, the court made the following comment:

> Now we have the government prosecuting registrants for failure to obey "interim orders." Despite the government's characterization of the order to report for a physical as interim, there appears to be a certain finality where the registrant is prosecuted and faces a prison sentence of up to five years for his failure to obey.

It was unfortunate that neither the *Unnasch* or the *Coyle* decisions were published and available to be cited by attorneys and other judges.

In addition to the cases noted during 1969 through 1970, Judge Lord found two more defendants not guilty, accepted one plea of guilty and found three additional defendants guilty. He presided over one jury trial, that of Dan Holland, a resister and activist with the Twin Cities Draft Information Center. Mr. Holland received a two-year sentence. That judgment was vacated when the Eighth Circuit remanded the case to the trial court following *Gutknecht.* He also sentenced Marvin Sagedahl to two years in prison and Steven Young to sixty days. Other defendants adjudicated guilty received probation and were required to perform twenty-four months of C.O. type employment.

Dan Holland's sentencing provides one of the few detailed records of Judge Lord's comments at sentencing. Holland was one of the organizers at the Twin Cities Draft Information Center. His sentencing was attended by about fifty of his friends and supporters, who stood behind him as he heard the judge sentence him to two years in prison for refusing induction. The judge warned those who came in with Holland that they would be removed if there were outbursts of laughter or comments. He said he would take their conduct "into consideration when I sentence Mr. Holland" as an indication of friends and background.

Holland's pre-sentencing remarks to the judge were short and pointed. "This sentence is not important. We're faced with much greater problems than going to jail. You should consider stepping off the bench and joining us. You don't stop war by sentencing draft resisters."

Judge Lord responded: "They usually call me judge, but you can call me mister. I find you to be a decent young man."

Lord recited a list of Holland's high school honors, including an American Legion citizenship award and a four-year scholarship from WCCO-TV. He concluded the list by saying he didn't think Holland "drinks to excess, smokes or drops acid" and criticized Holland's failure to seek a conscientious objector status:

> You have chosen instead to set yourself up as some sort of martyr. You've refused to compromise, you may call it patriotism. I call it very unfortunate for you, Dan Holland.

41

Lord also said that letting Holland out on probation only would "make a sham of these proceedings" because of his work with the Twin Cities Draft Information Center.

In January 1971, David Pence came before Judge Lord for the second time. After his conviction before Judge Devitt was reversed, Pence was given a C.O. classification and ordered to do C.O. work. When he refused the order, he was indicted. He was convicted by a jury; Judge Lord delayed a year before sentencing him to twelve months in prison. One other defendant who was convicted by a jury appeared before Judge Lord. He was sentenced to two months in jail.

Pence's present perspective is that Lord thought they were a bunch of traitors the first time around. In Pence's view, "Now he and his political buddies are against the war." Pence's recollection is that his father happened to be at some function in the suburbs where Judge Lord was a speaker. Lord referred to "this kid" who was in front of him who he knows is a good kid and he thought war was wrong . . . well everybody thinks the war is wrong now, says Lord. "What am I suppose to do? What should I do, should I send this kid to jail?"

Pence said he wrote a letter to Lord asking him to proceed, he said, "Please do the sentencing." At the sentencing Lord offered to discharge the guilty finding if Pence would do the alternative service. Pence refused and was sentenced to a year and a day. He spent his time in Sandstone and was discharged just before Christmas in 1972.

Later that year, Judge Lord sentenced a defendant to six months. He sent only one more defendant to jail for a draft related sentence during the Vietnam War era. All others adjudicated through pleas, court findings, or jury verdicts were placed on probation often with special conditions that the defendants do C.O. type work.

Judge Lord adjudicated ninety-four Selective Service cases during the Vietnam era. Of those, he had forty cases in 1972; eight cases in 1973; five cases in 1974, and one in 1975. In trials to the court in 1972 he found nine guilty and eleven not guilty. In 1973 through 1975 he had three court trials and found all three not guilty. As a result of guilty pleas and jury verdicts, he sentenced forty-one persons during the post 1972 era, none of whom received prison time. His most common sentence was twenty-four months on probation with a requirement that the person perform work similar to C.O. for a period of twenty-four months.

I was able to locate only five memorandum decisions written by Judge Lord in 1972, and one in 1973, none of which were published. In four of the decisions he acquitted the defendant. He convicted a young Jehovah's Witness who refused civilian work and had no serious challenge to the local board actions. The other four memorandums are interesting. Randolph Gonyer, a Jehovah's Witness, was denied a C.O. classification, refused induction and was indicted. The U.S. Attorney argued that the defendant was not "sincere" because he had been convicted four years before of possession of an alcoholic beverage by a minor and using an automobile without the owner's permission. The court cut to the chase quickly: There is no evidence that these incidents "were considered by the board to have had an effect on its decision . . ."

In a decision that I believe to be unique in Minnesota, Judge Lord was faced with a case involving a school teacher in rural Minnesota, Robert D. Ilse, whose superintendent requested a postponement of an induction order until the end of the school year. At the end of the school year, the local board sent the teacher a letter that his induction was "postponed until further notice." The teacher then filed a conscientious objector application form. The board sent Isle a new reporting date and refused to consider the C.O. claim on the grounds that the application was made after the original order to report for induction.

The issue was whether the original order had been "canceled" as a result of the two postponements. Judge Lord noted that the defendant did not request the postponements, but that they were requested by the school for the benefit of the school. He reviewed the regulations and the law on that question as well as the law relating to postponements that were for an "indefinite" period of time and not for a stated or defined period of time. Judge Lord held that an indefinite postponement is a cancellation. While the decision was unique in Minnesota, his holding clearly stated the majority and better reasoned rule. Thus the defendant was acquitted.

Judge Lord was also faced with a unique situation in a case where a young man's induction was "released per authority of state headquarters for enlistment." Apparently the defendant changed his mind and wrote the board requesting a C.O. application form. He received a letter from the clerk of the local board advising him that his claim could not be considered by the board because of his pending induction order.

Judge Lord found his induction was not "postponed" as they had taken no steps appropriate or necessary for a postponement, thus the order was canceled. He also found that the prosecution could not argue that the defendant did not in fact file a C.O. application. The action of the clerk prevented the defendant from filing the application. The defendant was acquitted.

Judge Lord also wrote an opinion in the case of Ricky Dean Ball, a young man who was married, had an eight-month-old child and was denied a hardship (IIIA) deferment. The file revealed no statement of reasons for the denial, and, as in the C.O. cases, the government claimed that there need not be a statement for reasons because the applicant had not filed a prima facie hardship claim. Judge Lord quickly disposed of the government's claim with quotations from the registrant and his wife that amply supported the claim.

It is difficult to generalize about the acts and statements of Judge Lord in selective service cases during the Vietnam War. I questioned him about his alleged statement at Pence and Gutknecht's first bail hearing in March of 1968. He said: "I probably did that." When I asked him about his statements in open court in 1972 that defendants could step up, plead guilty and go on their way, his answer was the same, "I did that." Whether one accepts David Pence's view that Judge Lord was merely following the winds of his "political buddies" or not, it is clear that Judge Lord did not have a firm and consistent judicial attitude toward draft cases and draft case defendants during the war. His record of acquittals and sentencing when compared to the other members of the Minnesota bench was, from the point of view of defendants, clearly much better. But, like his brethren, he gave the most severe sentences to vocal draft resisters, and the few memoranda he wrote seemed to be authored by persons having contradictory attitudes toward examining the law in selective service cases.

Some readers of this work might conclude that he was the "best" judge during the Vietnam era. That might be true, but it conjures up to me the historical conclusion that "the best and the brightest" were those who brought us the Vietnam disaster and then could not figure a way out.

Chapter Five

Judge Edward J. Devitt

> **"Have I heard you out counsel?"**
> *Judge Devitt's oft-repeated statement to counsel before ruling against the counsel to whom the question was directed.*

S ome observers believe that Judge Lord on occasion acted in an arbitrary manner, but it is a matter of perspective. Transcripts of hearings I reviewed show remarkable restraint. As a result of Judge Lord's removing himself from the cases, Pence and Gutknecht would have each of their cases heard by Judge Edward Devitt. The term "arbitrary" may take on a new definition.

Slightly more than one month from the date Judge Lord removed himself from the case, David Pence's case came up before Judge Devitt for trial. Dave Pence elected to have a jury trial; he wanted the jury to pass judgment on the war in Vietnam. The trial took place on April 30, 1968. Pence was convicted. On July 31, 1968, Judge Devitt denied a motion to set aside the jury verdict. In denying the post verdict motion, Judge Devitt stated, as he had previously, that he had a very limited power to review the "basis of fact" for the local board's action, that it was doubtful that even that limited review was available because Pence did not appeal the local board's action to the state appeal board. He founded his view on a 1946 World War II decision and noted the following as sufficient basis for the local board's actions:

> Pence indicated that he had no religious affiliation on his C.O. form. Pence stated in May 1967 that he would accept civilian work in lieu of induction. In October 1967 he stated he would not cooperate with an evil law, which "may be viewed as demonstrating an instability of beliefs and principles." His C.O. claim was filed long after his original registration and more than a year after he left the seminary and shortly before his 2-S classification (employment, i.e. VISTA deferment.)

Judge Devitt quoted from David Pence's written statements in his file and opined:

> They reflect an objection to the Vietnam War as immoral and to the draft as discriminatory. . . [this] may have been viewed by the local board as evidence of an absence of sincere conscientious to all wars.

He noted further that:

> Defendant's belated claim for conscientious objector status coincided with the increase in anti-Vietnam demonstrations.

Judge Devitt's final conclusion was:

> I am satisfied that here is a basis in fact for the classification which the board gave this defendant.

He sentenced David Pence to three years in prison. Doug Hall filed an appeal. Pence has little recollection of the appeal. He doubts that he ever read the briefs. He is certain he did not attend oral argument and really wanted to get it over with. On May 1, 1969, the Court of Appeals handed down its decision reversing Judge Devitt with direction to enter a verdict of acquittal. Judge Donald Lay wrote the opinion for the Appellate Panel.

> His [Pence's] speech relating to civil disobedience and opposition to the Selective Service laws as well as the Vietnam War does not detract from his previous statement reflecting his deep religious objection to serve in the military and bear arms. The First Amendment protects a conscien-

tious objector as well as anyone else to the right of free speech and the right to dissent.

The only basis this record affords of Pence's reclassification to 1-A are lawless reasons.

The court concluded as follows:

It is well recognized that religious principles do not justify any person becoming a law unto himself or to defy the enlightened sentiments of mankind. . . . If religious scruples drive men to civil or criminal disobedience in a society of law, the state is "supreme within it's sphere and submission or punishment follows. . . ." However, any meaningful society based upon law strives to recognize those principles of individual conscience within reasonable bounds and to make meaningful the

Judge Edward Devitt. (Courtesy of the Minnesota Historical Society)

integrity of spiritual values to every extent possible without conflict with the public need. Congress has so enacted certain exemptions within the Selective Service laws. *If these laws may be thwarted by reasons of mere refusals to acquiesce in an alleged "voluntary" act requested by a local board or because officials of the state disagree with a selectee's political views, then we substitute government of the men for government of laws. This we refuse to do.*

David Gutknecht's trial before Judge Devitt took place on May 9, 1968. David was represented by Chester Bruvold. Bruvold, like many of the early defendants, was a member of the local Society of Friends, i.e. Quakers. Early on, Bruvold was the only attorney in Minnesota with any extensive experience in defending Selective Service cases. Ultimately he played a significant part in many cases. Among the early high visibility cases he handled, in addition to *Gutknecht*, were cases for Seth Peterson, Fran Shor, John Seman, and Rolf Kolden. Gutknecht waived a jury trial, and the case was tried to the court. Judge Devitt found Gutknecht guilty on May 9, 1968.

Bruvold had a tendency to raise issues that seemed trivial and ill conceived, and he did so in Gutknecht's case. Judge Devitt testily disposed of such issues. But Bruvold also argued that the regulation authorizing a person to be declared delinquent was unconstitutional and that he was indicted because of the memoranda and letters by Selective Service Director Hershey to local draft boards to induct registrants participating in anti-Vietnam demonstrations.

Devitt's responses to the issues were as follows:

> There is nothing in the Selective Service file or any of the evidence received at trial to support the assertion that defendant's classification as a delinquent and orders to report for induction were based on his expressions of opposition to the Vietnam War. But, on the contrary, it appears that the action of the Selective Service Board was based on the defendant's violation of the regulations that he have the draft cards in his possession at all times.
>
> *O'Brien* vs. *The United States* upheld the constitutionality of the regulations authorizing a Selective Service Board to declare delinquent and order the induction of persons found to be without possession of the required Selective Service cards.
>
> There is no evidence in the record that shows the defendant was declared delinquent and ordered to report for induction by authority of the so-called Hershey Amendment.

Judge Devitt sentenced Gutknecht to four years in prison.

Pence and Gutknecht were sentenced by Judge Devitt at the same time. Pence received a three-year sentence, Gutknecht four years. Gutknecht believes it was because of the way they appeared. Pence, suburban, clean cut, polite, friendly, even wholesome. Gutknecht, rural, unkempt, scruffy, surly, perhaps disrespectful. I wonder if Pence's Catholic background and education played a major role? Judge Devitt remained active in Catholic church activities his entire life.

Judge Devitt's decision in *Gutknecht* fared a little better than his decision in *Pence.*

On the morning of March 31, 1966, David O'Brien and three companions burned their Selective Service registration cards on the steps of the South Boston courthouse. In 1965 an act of Congress amending the Selective Service Act made such conduct a federal crime. On appeal from O'Brien's conviction, the Court of Appeals for the First Circuit held the provision unconstitutional. In January of 1968, the United States Supreme Court disagreed and reinstated the conviction. It did hold that Congress had the power to pass a law making it a federal offense to burn a draft card, but they did *not* state that the Selective Service could punish a registrant who burned, turned in, or failed to keep his card. They said the opposite.

At the time Judge Devitt decided the Gutknecht case, the delinquency regulations were under heavy attack. Attorneys in the Department of Justice were urging Director of Selective Service Hershey to cool down his rhetoric attacking antiwar registrants and to withdraw his letter to the local boards to move quickly in the case of public antidraft, antiwar activists who became delinquent by turning in their draft cards. It was clear that some in the Department of Justice felt that the regulation permitting reclassification of a delinquent was not authorized by the Selective Service Act and might be thus illegal. The case of a divinity student, James J. Oestereich, was making its way through the courts. Oestereich sought to enjoin the draft board from taking away his divinity student deferment (IV-D) on the ground that he had returned his draft card and was delinquent.

On December 16, 1968, the United States Supreme Court decided *Oestereich,* found the regulation permitting reclassification because the registrant had turned in his card, "lawless" and granted an injunction. The only dissents were from the grant of a pre-induction injunction.

Oestereich did not decide the question of whether or not the delinquency regulation could be used to accelerate an induction order as in Gutknecht, but it heightened doubts about the matter. The Department of Justice argued that order of call, unlike classification, was exclusively a matter for the Selective Service boards and that Congress left the order of call questions to the Selective Service System.

Bruvold obtained the services of Mike Tiger to brief and argue the case in the Supreme Court. Tiger was one of the founders and editors of the *Selective Service Law Review,* which had rapidly become the authoritative work in the field and required reading for all practitioners. He was then a young law professor at Stanford Law School. He is now widely recognized as one of the premier criminal defense trial attorneys in the country and teaches law at the University of Texas Law School.

The Court of Appeals for the Eighth Circuit addressed the specific issues raised by Bruvold and distinguished *Gutknecht* from *Oestereich* on the grounds that *Oestereich* involved a classification issue; *Gutknecht* involved an accelerated induction order. It found no objection to the use of the regulation for this more limited purpose.

Justice Douglas delivered the opinion of the Supreme Court on January 19, 1970:

> Among the defenses tendered at this trial was the legality of the delinquency regulations which were applied to petitioner. It is that single question that we will consider.
>
> The power under the regulations to declare a registrant "delinquent" has no statutory standard or even guidelines. The power is exercised entirely at the discretion of the local board. It is a broad, roving authority, a type of administrative absolutism not congenial to our law-making traditions.

The court found that the regulations were outside the powers of the Selective Service Board under the laws passed by Congress. There were several short concurring comments but no dissents. Mr. Justice Stewart, concurring in the judgment, would not have reached the issued because he found the local board act lawless in ordering Gutknecht for induction five days after they declared him delinquent.

Were Judge Devitt's decisions in *Pence* and *Gutknecht* aberrations? Clearly the answer is no. Judge Devitt tried forty-two non-jury Selective Service cases. He found thirty-one guilty. That's a conviction rate of seventy-four percent, the highest among the four judges studied. He sentenced fifty-two Selective Service defendants; that included eleven found guilty after jury verdict and ten who plead guilty. Of the fifty-two sentenced, he sent twenty-three to jail for an average jail sentence several times as severe as his colleagues. The details are set forth in the Appendix attached. Significantly, Judge Devitt had eleven cases appealed. He was reversed six times; that is more reversals than the other three judges in the district combined.

Judge Devitt was born on May 5, 1911, in St. Paul, Minnesota, in the Dayton's Bluff neighborhood. He attended elementary school with Warren Burger and Henry Blackmun, who were to become chief justice and associate justice of the United States Supreme Court. His father was a roundhouse fireman for the CSM & O Railway. He graduated from St. John's College in Collegeville, Minnesota, and obtained a law degree from the University of North Dakota Law School. He worked for the Minnesota Attorney General and was commissioned in the Navy as a lieutenant commander serving from 1942 to 1945. Injured, he received a Purple Heart. In 1946 he again worked for the Attorney General until his successful run for election to Congress. He served one term as a Republican member of Congress, was defeated by Eugene McCarthy in 1948, and St. Paul has not been represented by a Republican in the U.S. House of Representatives of the United States Congress since his term. Devitt practiced briefly in St. Paul, was appointed a probate judge in Ramsey County in 1950, and four years later he was nominated by President Eisenhower to the federal bench. He took senior status on his seventieth birthday in 1981 and died on March 3, 1992.

Devitt always looked as if he was assigned by Hollywood central casting to play the role of federal judge. He had a chiseled Irish face, with wavy hair, and certainly could be charming. He was generous with his time in various charitable groups, particularly around Christmas.

I think it is not unfair to say that Devitt was the preferred judge of prosecuting attorneys, personal injury defense attorneys, and corporate counsel. He was given most every honor that the press and establishment bar could give a judge. One thing he never received, however, was the respect and affection as a judge by those who appeared on "the other side" of counsel table.

He was a co-author of *Federal Jury Practice and Instructions* and the person honored by West Publishing Company's Edward J. Devitt Distinguished Service Award. But many remember him less fondly as a judge committed more to judicial speed and convenience than to concepts of justice or equity. He introduced and championed the six-person jury, and he supported eliminating the civil jury in federal court. His innovative way of jury selection was simple. He called all the jurors to the courthouse and all the attorneys whose case might be heard in the ensuing weeks or months, and case-by-case, each set of attorneys selected a jury and went back to their office to await a call to come to trial. It was quick and efficient. No sole practitioner or small law firm could possibly practice law with one foot out the door at any moment to start a federal trial. Only the major firms could possibly handle the problems created, but it presented no problem for the court. While he clearly was not a favorite of criminal defense attorneys, he was not considered a tough sentencer.

Judge Devitt often walked the sidewalks and the skyways of St. Paul, and on several occasions we walked together. I knew him from the time he was a probate judge until shortly before his death. Outside of court, he called me "Kenny" which I found more than a little disconcerting because we were never close, and no one I knew ever called me "Kenny." For years he referred to longtime Federal Public Defender Scott Tilsen as my son. He's my nephew.

In the later years of his retirement, I stopped correcting him. Every attorney I know told of the judge's habit of asking counsel, "Have

I heard you out?" He followed any affirmative response with an adverse ruling. I had a few experiences that give some insight into the court. Up until sometime in 1974, the Minnesota Federal Courts had no office of Community or Public Defender. The federal judges would each appoint attorneys from a list developed by that judge. The judge's former law clerks often made up the bulk of the lists. I have never been on such a list.

As the number of Selective Service cases escalated in late 1971 and early 1972, I helped organize and administer an informal group of attorneys willing to take appointments in these cases. We developed a "brief bank" and other resources and let the word out to many attorneys that we were able and willing to help them on these cases. Our work came to the attention of Judges Larson and Neville, and, with their approval, I drew up a list of attorneys willing to accept appointments. I was appointed several times by Judges Larson and Neville and many times asked to take specific, troublesome Selective Service cases. In early 1972, I received a call from Judge Devitt to accept an appointment in a check-forgery case. I was particularly busy at the time. I did not turn it down, but I did ask him why he turned to me for the appointment. His answer conveyed a clear message: "I hear you hold yourself out as having some special expertise in Selective Service cases. You must have extra time on your hand. I believe that every attorney is capable of handling every case."

That was the only time I was ever appointed by Judge Devitt. But, I did accept an invitation from Judge Neville to serve as volunteer advisor counsel to Judge Devitt's son-in-law's brother who walked out of his Rochester, Minnesota, draft board with his draft file and threw it in the nearest rubbish can.

The Minnesota Eight

On July 11, 1970, eight persons were arrested as a result of three separate late-night entries in draft boards in Winona, Alexandria, and Little Falls, Minnesota. The F.B.I. had been forewarned and, along with local police, had secreted themselves in and around the draft boards before any records were damaged.

> The FBI Agents had been hiding in the darkened storage room for perhaps three hours when breaking glass announced the midnight arrival of intruders at the U.S. Selective Service office in Winona, last Friday night.
>
> *Minneapolis Tribune*, July 17, 1970.

The agents hiding in the storage room and in a trailer parked across the street from the Winona draft office waited until they heard metal pounding on metal before presenting themselves and arresting Donald Olson, Brad Beneke, and Peter Simmons.

Seven F.B.I. agents, assisted by four Alexandria policemen, arrested William Tilton, Charles Turchick, and Clifton Ulen at the Alexandria draft board around midnight after they pried open a file cabinet.

In Little Falls, Minnesota, at about the same time, Francis Kronke and Michael Therriault were arrested by agents who hid in a lawyer's office. Apparently they had succeeded in entering the draft board and breaking the typewriter keys for the number "1" and the letter "A." All of the defendants were young men from the Twin Cities. That same evening all 1A files were removed from the draft board in Wabasha, Minnesota. The Wabasha records were later found along the banks of the Mississippi River in St. Paul. The defendants became known as the "Minnesota 8."

They were originally held on a charge of interfering with national defense under the sabotage statute but were indicted on September 23, 1970 for interfering with the Selective Service by attempting to destroy Selective Service records.

There were three separate indictments. Two were assigned to Judge Devitt. The third was assigned to Judge Neville. I represented all of the defendants except Cliff Ulen who pled guilty. It is widely assumed that Ulen informed on the others. However, that assumption is based solely on his guilty plea and a sentence of probation. The group's plans could have been detected in other ways.

Each trial was interesting, although all the defendants were convicted, and each sentenced to a term of five years. The pace of prosecution was remarkable, almost unbelievably fast, but it was not unusual for Judge Devitt. Following the indictments, he denied all motions for discovery and attacks upon the pleading and set the trials to begin on November 4, 1970, less than three weeks after the arraignment. The first trial was for the remaining Alexandria defendants, Tilton and Turchick. It began on November 3 and concluded with a guilty verdict on the fifth. Sentencing was set for December 28, 1970. The trial of the Winona defendants Olson, Beneke, and Simmons began on November 17, 1970. On the eighteenth, a mistrial was declared when several jurors were overheard discussing the case in the courthouse cafeteria. The retrial started on November 30th, and the jury verdict was returned on December 2, 1970.

No record can be found of anyone publicly referring to Judge Devitt as "Speedy Eddie" but that was the name given him by many defendants and attorneys. The sentence of five years for each of the Minnesota Eight defendants was not surprising. Bill Tilton addressed the court in his own behalf at sentencing. He advised Harry Berglund, Chief U.S. Marshall, that he would have been a good S.S. Trooper; as to the judge, he told him he was simply a good German—he was doing his job. Brad Beneke had been grabbed by marshalls for not rising for the court while a spectator at an earlier draft resister's trial. When Beneke protested his imminent removal, he was brought before the judge, who refused to respond to his request for an explanation. He then called Judge Devitt a "pompous ass" and was sentenced to ten days in jail. Judge Devitt denied motions to recuse himself from Beneke's trial based on the incident.

Wounded Knee

My personal comments about Judge Devitt would not be complete without some reference to the trial of Russell Means and Dennis Banks arising out of the events at Wounded Knee in February through May of 1973. The Eighth Circuit Court of appeals moved the trial from

South Dakota to Minnesota on our motion. Judge Fred Nichol of Rapid City presided. The trial drew national publicity. Hundreds of Indian people traveled to Minnesota to observe the trial and to support the defendants. Trial started in January 1974 and ended in October. At the beginning, we were observers in a turf battle between Judge Nichol and Judge Devitt. It began when Judge Nichol ordered pay telephones installed in the existing telephone booths in the courthouse corridor for the use of public and the press. Judge Devitt entered an order that no work of any kind could be done in the courthouse without his consent. The prosecution and F.B.I. took over almost the entire second floor of the courthouse as a "command center" and to deal with the tens of thousands of exhibits. Judge Nichol assigned the defense team two unused rooms on the courtroom floor. U.S. Marshall Berglund barred our entry at Judge Devitt's insistence. In the end Judge Nichol got his way. He said that he ordered his marshall to arrest Berglund the next time he interfered with his, Judge Nichols', orders. I always thought that Judge Nichol was kidding, but maybe not. I do know that for the entire nine months of the trial, both Judge Devitt and Harry Berglund seemed to disappear from the courthouse.

In 1969 and 1970, Judge Devitt had only five court-tried, i.e. non-jury, Selective Service trials. The only defendant not found guilty by the court was Brian Coyle. This was Coyle's first indictment. Coyle's induction order had been accelerated when he sent back his draft card. On February 1970, after the Supreme Court reversed Devitt's conviction of Gutknecht, Judge Devitt had no choice but to dismiss Coyle's indictment. That same year the U.S. Attorney indicted Coyle for not taking his physical. In December 1970, Judge Lord threw out that case.

Judge Devitt presided over several jury trials during this period. In addition to the five defendants convicted by Judge Devitt arising out of the "Minnesota Eight" trials, Judge Devitt had one more jury trial in which the defendant was convicted.

The only case that resulted in a memorandum by Judge Devitt in 1969 and 1970 was a court trial in which I represented George

Crocker's younger brother. John, a nineteen-year-old Quaker refused to register on religious grounds. Judge Devitt treated it as an attack on the constitutionality of the draft, although we argued much more than that. He responded to our argument as follows:

> If defendant's view were accepted, a person's mere assertion of conscientious objection would foreclose any inquiring into it, and those who become subject to registration could avoid the law by merely asserting conscientious objection without being required to make a showing of it.

While Judge Devitt's argument seems to fall by itself without the need for more than a slight push, the fact is no court has supported religious conviction as a defense to the crime of failure to register.

Judge Devitt sentenced Crocker to three years of probation provided he would perform two years of C.O.-type work. John agreed to perform the C.O.-type work, but within the month proceedings were brought to revoke his probation on the grounds that he still hadn't registered for the draft. We objected strongly to the revocation. Judge Devitt revoked his probation and ordered him to prison for three years.

On appeal, the Court of Appeals for the Eighth Circuit *reversed* the parole revocation. After noting the undisputed evidence of the defendant's willingness to comply with the prescribed work conditions, the Appellate Court wrote:

> . . . it appears obvious that defendant would refuse to register for the draft . . . if at the time of the entry of the probation order the court had any doubt about this, it could have been readily resolved by a question directed to defendant. It would appear pointless to impose the unique condition of performing work of national importance if the court intended to make the probation conditional upon draft registration.

The court held that the probation revocation was an abuse of the court's discretion.

During 1969 and 1970, in addition to the Minnesota Eight cases, Judge Devitt sentenced five others: two received twenty-four-month prison sentences, and three received thirty-six-month probation on condition they perform twenty-four months of C.O.-type work. One of the defendants, Seth Peterson, an early resister, was put on probation on condition he perform twenty-four months of C.O.-type work. He refused, and his probation was revoked. He was resentenced to two years in prison. This was the second indictment of Seth. His first indictment was dismissed when they discovered his order for indictment was issued five days after he was classified 1A.

Judge Devitt found one defendant not guilty in a court trial in 1971; six defendants were found guilty. He sentenced four others who plead guilty.

Terrance Peterson was denied a C.O. classification by the board. When he received his 1A classification from the local board, he wrote back as follows:

> Obviously this is a mistake, since, according to the supplement supplied with the classification card, 1A denotes that the registrant is available for military service. The recipient of this card, namely me, is not now and never will be available for such service. He also wrote the board after he received his induction order "resigning from the system."

The Court of Appeals (Judge Lay) pointed out that the actions quoted by Judge Devitt were irrelevant to the question of his classification. They took place after he was classified and were not in his file. The appellate court noted the inappropriate nature of the justification given by the trial court and cited *Pence* and *Gutknecht*, both tried by Judge Devitt and reversed on appeal for the propositions that distasteful and inappropriate actions, contumacious acts of civil dissent or expletives should not foreclose an objective evaluation. It footnoted Justice Douglas in *Gutknecht*. "Nor do we read the act as granting personal privileges that may be forfeited for transgressions that affront the local board."

During the entire Vietnam Era Judge Devitt adjudicated sixty-one cases, twenty-four in the 1968 to 1971 period and thirty-seven in 1972 and later years. He sentenced twenty-eight persons in the post 1971 period; ten to jail time mostly for six or twelve months. Nonetheless as evidenced by the comparison data in the Appendix, his sentences were considerably more harsh than the sentences of any of the other Minnesota Federal Court judges.

Judge Devitt wrote fourteen memoranda on Selective Service cases during the 1972 through 1975 period.

The first decision in 1972 in which Judge Devitt wrote a memorandum involved the denial of a teaching deferment (IIA) to David Bender.

Without discussing any of the facts, Judge Devitt noted that Mr. Bender did not appeal the board action, i.e., he did not exhaust his administrative remedy. Judge Devitt neither acknowledged nor discussed any of the cases or reasoning that precludes or permits a defense to be raised when a Selective Service defendant does not appeal the classification. "This is not a case where exceptional circumstances which would require a relaxation of the exhaustion doctrine have been shown."

The issue is whether Bender on August 19, 1969, was a registrant who "is, or but for a seasonal interruption would be engaged" in teaching. The question was whether Bender was entitled to the teaching deferment during the summer when school was not in session. The local board interpreted the regulations to deny the deferment unless the registrant was actually teaching.

The Court of Appeals noted that the defendant had directed telephone calls and letters to the board challenging that interpretation. It isn't so much that Devitt was wrong on the issue, but so far as the record shows he never recognized the question. The conviction of Mr. Bender was reversed. As to the proper interpretation of the teaching deferment regulation, the Court of Appeals directed the reader to Judge Larson's opinion in the case of Timothy Olmscheid.

The Court of Appeals also noted that in a case involving the proper interpretation of a regulation, the registrant need not appeal the local board action to the state Selective Service Appeal board.

In March of 1972, Judge Devitt sentenced Karl Burton for a year in prison for failing to keep his local board advised of his address and refusing induction. Burton had been convicted by a jury. At trial the evidence showed that the local board in fact had Burton's mother's address and further that the local board had given Burton misleading and erroneous information regarding his right to file for a C.O. classification.

Judge Devitt had refused to grant a requested instruction regarding the erroneous C.O. information and had denied post-trial dismissal motions.

The Court of Appeals ruled that as a matter of law the defendant was not guilty of failing to keep the local board advised of his address.

It also granted a new trial because Devitt did not properly instruct the jury and admonished the court and prosecution as follows:

> On this record the government may seem to have little chance of overcoming (defendant's) evidence, but that is a matter of prosecutorial evaluation of other evidence.

Other published short, superficial decisions authored by Judge Devitt in this time period include the cases of Frank Robinson and James Roda. Robinson may well have had a valid C.O. claim although it is difficult to tell from the judge's memo. It is not clear that Roda had any serious defense. Judge Devitt wrote a memorandum in the case of Jerry Schaefer that provides some insight into the judge's thinking.

At issue were the interpretation of regulations that define priority induction and the operation of the random sequence number system. The priority group for a registrant whose number had been reached but who had not been given a pre-induction physical or an order to report for induction is designated as the "extended priority selection group." The court did not agree with the defendant's reading of the regulation and cited no cases either for or against the defendant's argument. What the court did do was cite a 1939 and a 1946 decision of the Second Circuit during World War II that had nothing to do with the subject before the court but cautioned that the court should not

> . . . find technical construction which is not necessary for the protection of the rights of the individual and which merely results in hampering the government.

Further insight into Judge Devitt is gained from the judge's memorandum decision convicting Donald Babcock. Mr. Babcock was indicted on January 20, 1972. On April 5, 1972, Judge Devitt convicted Mr. Babcock, who had requested a ministerial exemption (IVD) as a Jehovah's Witness. Judge Devitt acknowledged that the board gave no reason for its actions but relied upon the case of Captain Oliver Fein in the Supreme Court for the alleged rule that in September 1971, the law did not require the local board to state a reason for its acts. In 1971 Congress amended the Selective Service Regulations and provided registrants substantial new rights. The new regulations also required a statement of reasons for local and appeal board actions. The *Fein* case held that the new regulations were not necessarily retroactive.

The best that can be said for Judge Devitt's conviction of Babcock is that the *Fein* case does absolutely compel a contrary result. Judge Devitt stated that

> . . . after September 2, 1971, it is required that the board furnish a brief written statement of the reasons for its decision regardless of whether or not the registrant makes a prima facie showing of qualification.

The 1971 act of Congress to which Judge Devitt referred and the U.S. Supreme Court in *Fein* granted Selective Service registrants the right to a personal appearance and the right to testify and to present evidence before the local and appeal boards.

The history of the legislative change and the many cases which held that due process required a statement of reasons by the board all argue in favor of compelling a statement of reasons before September 2, 1971.

Fein was an action for affirmative relief against the Selective Service system alleging that the administrative procedures involved in his case violated due process. The majority decision held simply that they would not use this case to expand the scope of pre-induction review set forth in the Supreme Court decisions in *Oestereich, Clark* v. *Gabriel* and *Breen.*

The *Fein* court notes the serious due-process problem that the new regulations were designed to solve and states quite clearly that if Dr. Fein were before it on review of his 1968 induction order and refusal to submit to induction in a criminal case, due process would require his acquittal.

It is absurd to convict a man of a felony based on action by a draft board that has been declared by the courts to be a violation of due process on the basis that Congressional action changing the procedure is not expressly retroactive. It also reflects a failure to look at the law with care. Unfortunately, that failure is also evident in other decisions of Judge Devitt.

Not all of Judge Devitt's decisions were convictions. In June of 1972 he acquitted two defendants. One involved Jay Huntsiger that I represented in a court trial. Mr. Huntsiger filed a well-supported and documented C.O. claim. However, he failed to appeal the denial of his claim to the state board. In a memo-decision of June 2, 1972, Judge Devitt found that the registrant's failure to appeal may have been caused by defects in the Selective Service system at the time of his classification, and thus it would not be proper to apply the exhaustion doctrine. He found Mr. Huntsiger not guilty.

Rodger Kiemele's case came up before Judge Devitt later that month. Mr. Kiemele had submitted a C.O. petition that was denied without a statement of reasons. In a short decision, Judge Devitt found that the absence of a statement of reasons was a fatal flaw in the process requiring a judgment of acquittal. The opposite decisions by Judge Devitt in *Babcock* and *Kiemele* is bewildering.

Judge Devitt also acquitted two separate defendants in cases where the draft board, through their own errors, neglected to send a notice of induction to persons in the "Extended Priority Group" prior to April 1, 1971. The regulations provided that persons in that group must be inducted by April first unless excused pursuant to certain conditions in the regulations.

I found these two unusual decisions to be unique and very well reasoned and supported. Surprisingly neither of these latter two decisions were reported. It might provide some insight into Judge Devitt to discover why he did *not* send these two decisions for publication.

Finally, I note two very similar cases with opposite results. In May of 1972, Judge Devitt found Jeffery Johnson guilty of refusing induction. The defendant filed a C.O. claim after he received a notice of induction. Various postponements of induction were granted at the request of the defendant. Judge Devitt simply noted that reopening was foreclosed by the law once an order to report to induction was sent and thus he convicted Mr. Johnson.

I represented the second case of Stanley E. Willet, whose case I contrast with Johnson's. On June 16, 1970, the local board mailed Willet an order to report for induction in July 6, 1970. Willet requested a Form 150 (C.O. application) on June 18, 1970, two days after the order to report was sent. He completed and returned it. He refused induction in July 1970. Judge Devitt found that Willet's application met all the requirements of the law and that "the government did not question the sincerity of defendant's beliefs at trial, other than noting that defendant filed his C.O. claim after he was ordered to report."

The court found the defendant's demeanor at trial to be thoughtful and sincere and there was no basis in fact for the denial of his request. Therefore, he was not guilty.

Let there be no question about it. The judge who seemed unable or unwilling to apply generally accepted principles of due process to Selective Service cases, or to recognize that the world had changed since World War II, and who continued to outpace his confederates on the bench in rate of convictions and sentence severity was capable of quirky, unique decisions when he chose to do so. When the need arose he could simply ignore the facts and the law and acquit those whose cases met his undisclosed personal standards in much the same manner that he convicted defendants who had a substantial defense to the charge at hand.

Chapter Six

Judge Larson

"The decision is . . . outside the competency of the judiciary."
    Judge Larson in denying relief in an action brought by the State of Minnesota to enjoin sending Minnesotans to Vietnam in an undeclared war.

In October of 1969, Scott Alarik was indicted shortly after his eighteenth birthday for failing to register. His case was assigned to Judge Larson. Along with Alarik, I accompanied a large group of clergymen and college professors to a meeting with the U.S. Attorney Robert Renner. At the meeting, each person present "confessed" to having aided, abetted, advised, and counseled Alarik to violate the law and not register. Further, each stated that they have agreed and conspired with each other, and each gave and exchanged material support to Alarik and each other. Finally in the presence of the U.S. Attorney, each handed money to Alarik to aid and abet him and in furtherance of their conspiracy.

Representing Alarik, I brought a motion to dismiss based on age discrimination in enforcement of the Selective Service Laws. It was clear

On March 5, 1969, during services at the Universalist Church in Minneapolis, sixteen young men signed a letter declaring that they refused to register for the draft. Scott Alarik stands at the right facing the audience. (Photo by Krueger, from the *Minneapolis Star-Tribune* News Negative Collection, courtesy of the Minnesota Historical Society)

that only those young persons subject directly to the draft were prosecuted. Judge Earl Larson heard our evidence and motion on December 10, 1969. We produced a series of witnesses and called U.S. Attorney Renner to the stand to prove his knowledge of our collective illegal acts.

Renner testified that he took into account the unpopularity of the draft laws as one of the many factors he considered in deciding to prosecute draft violations under the aiding and abetting sections. Basically he said the witnesses were simply exercising their right of freedom to speak.

On February 26, 1970, Judge Larson entered his decision, and Scott Alarik was found guilty. Judge Larson found that the witnesses were not in the same situation as the defendant. Their charge would be under different sections of the law and thus may be treated differently. He found the actions of the U.S. Attorney within his discretion and sentenced Alarik to three years on probation on condition that he register within ten days and spend twenty-four months of employment "in the national interest."

Alarik did not register, and on April 5, 1971, Larson revoked his probation, and the sentence was executed. The Court of Appeals affirmed both the guilty finding and the revocation of probation.

John Crocker had been tried and convicted before Judge Devitt for failing to register on February 11, 1970, and sentenced on March 30, 1970, shortly after Alrick was sentenced. He was

Judge Earl Larson. (Courtesy of the Minnesota Historical Society)

also given a three-year prison term suspended on condition he perform two years of work in the public interest. Devitt did not make registration a condition of probation. Crocker, like Alarik did not register, and Devitt revoked his probation over our objections. On appeal, the Eighth Circuit agreed that Judge Devitt could not revoke his probation for not registering because it had not been made a condition of his probation. Thus, two young men in almost identical circumstances both represented by me were convicted of non-registration, but only one went to jail.

During the Vietnam War period, Judge Earl Larson handled more Selective Service cases than any other Minnesota judge. He had sixty-nine of those cases tried to him without a jury and found fifty, or seventy-two percent, guilty. Only Judge Devitt with seventy-four percent guilty had a higher conviction rate. Judge Larson had no jury trials although all the other judges had several (Devitt —eleven, Neville—nine, and Lord—six). Larson also sentenced twenty-seven persons who pled guilty before him for a total of seventy-eight sentenced. Of those seventy-eight, he sent thirty, or over thirty-eight percent, to jail. The only judge to sentence fewer to jail was Judge Lord. Judge Larson's median sentence was six months, the same as Judges Lord and Neville. The exact details are all set forth in the appendix attached hereto.

Judge Larson was born in Minneapolis on December 18, 1911. Like Judge Devitt, one sometimes has the feeling that Larson was born a federal judge, and all other descriptions are irrelevant. But that may be all they have in common. Every encounter with Judge Larson, in and out of the courtroom, formally or casually is memorable. One is impressed with his calm, almost humble, yet commanding presence, his clear and precise habit of language and indeed his intellect.

Earl Larson grew up in Minneapolis, graduated from North High, attended the University of Minnesota where he was president of the All University Student Council, captain of the golf team and a cum laude graduate. Classmate and friend Eric Severoid described him as "the prime leader of our little gang of political marauders," but I could not discover what they did to justify the title. After graduating law school at Minnesota, he practiced law privately for several years before becoming an assistant U.S. Attorney. He was an officer in the Army from 1942 until the end of World War II. Judge Larson married Cecil Holmgren in 1939. They are still married. He has a son, Dick, who was an attorney for the ACLU in its New York headquarters, and a daughter who teaches English in Spain.

His most memorable pre-judicial event was the formation of a law firm in Minneapolis that nurtured the origins of the Democratic

Farmer Labor Party in Minnesota and fertilized it with a long list of political leaders, judges, and dignitaries. The law firm of Larson and Lindquist included in its membership Orville Freeman (governor of the state of Minnesota and United States secretary of agriculture), Walter Mondale (vice-president and U.S. senator), Donald Fraser (U.S. House of Representatives and mayor of Minneapolis), Henry MacLaughlin (federal judge—District of Minnesota), along with many other people important in the political and intellectual life of Minnesota.

Judge Larson handled a long list of important complex litigations that included overseeing school desegregation for over a decade. He made significant decisions involving reapportionment, affirmative action, mental health standards, due process for student athletes, antitrust laws, and securities law.

In 1971, the State of Minnesota enacted a statute authorizing the attorney general to challenge orders to send Minnesota residents to Vietnam in the absence of a Declaration of War. The case was brought and, I thought, pursued rigorously.

Judge Larson, not surprisingly, refused to enjoin the pending order sending a Minnesota resident to Vietnam. He did so not because he believed that the war was right but because:

> the decision is one of policy and is committed to the discretion of the Congress and is outside the competency of the judiciary. . . .

His decision was clearly in accordance with most, if not all, similar cases at the time. But one has to wonder, what makes a court capable of running a school system or defining mental hospital rules and practices yet somehow incompetent to stop young men being sent to slaughter or to be slaughtered?

When I visited with Judge Larson and interviewed him on July 25, 1999, I found him physically quite infirm but mentally sharp. He was very giving and open. I showed him the results of my research, and he commented several times on the significant sentencing differences between the judges. He stated that he was keenly aware that there were judges in other parts of the country who gave every person convicted of draft violation five years and others who gave them no sentence. He mentioned St. Louis as an example of the former and San Francisco as an example of the latter. He expressed surprise that Judge Neville sent so many more than he did to prison. "I guess I was aware of sentencing discrepancies around the country, but I never thought about it in our district." He was quite certain that the judges never met to discuss the handling of draft cases but acknowledged that when they did have occasion to meet, at lunch or over coffee, the war would be the major topic of conversation. He indicated without hesitation that they exchanged opinions on the war and its progress.

"By 1970 and 1971, there was increased skepticism as to any valid reason to continue the war. The losses were tremendous, 58,000 soldiers. It certainly affected public opinion."

"Did it affect the courts?"

"That's hard to say. We all kept track of the war. The progress."

"Were you aware of any changes in your colleagues?"

"Not really, no."

He completed that part of the interview as follows: "I suppose the logical thing is to discover what's happening locally but I never did, so we'll be happy to read your paper, what we all did, it will be interesting."

After commenting again on the difference between the St. Louis and San Francisco judges he offered: "Discrepancies like that aren't good but the effort to solve them has created worse problems. The courts have got to change. We cannot continue to put so many minority people in jail; guidelines are good but absolute rules created more problems than they solved."

In 1968 Judge Larson had two draft cases before him who pled guilty and each received twenty-four-month sentences. One of those cases was Mark Suchy, whose case I mentioned earlier when Judge Larson noted that he was sure he would continue to make a major contribution to the community. The other was John Samborski who was also an antiwar resister.

In 1969 Judge Larson had four court trials before him; he found three not guilty and one guilty. He sentenced the guilty defendant to twenty-four months in prison.

The case of Timothy Hansen was unusual. Hansen registered at eighteen when he was still in high school. He advised the board at that time that he was totally deaf in one ear as a result of an accident. When he graduated from high school that June, he was classified 1A and ordered to report for a physical. He reported for the physical and was found "fit for military service." He furnished the local board additional letters from a medical specialist, and he was still found "qualified" and ordered to report for induction. He did not do so. A short time later he obtained and filed an application for Conscientious Objector status. The board did not consider the application.

The significant question before the court was whether Hansen's file should have been reopened to consider the C.O. application. Judge Larson quoted with approval the decision of the Second Circuit that:

> The realization that induction is pending and that he may soon be asked to take another's life may cause a young man to finally crystallize and articulate his once vague sentiments.

Larson ruled that, in this case, with the letter from an ear, nose and throat specialist in his file, the defendant had good cause to believe he would never have to serve in the Armed Forces. His C.O. position may well have matured after he received the notice for induction and thus the board must at least review the application. Mr. Hansen was found not guilty.

Also in 1969 Judge Larson found Fran Shor guilty and sentenced him to two years in prison. Execution of Shor's sentence was stayed pending appeal and a finding of not guilty entered on motion following the Supreme Court reversal of Dave Gutknecht.

In 1970, Judge Larsen adjudicated eleven cases. He found two not guilty, one pled guilty, and eight were found guilty.

Judge Larsen had no jury trials in Selective Service cases during the Vietnam War era.

During 1970, Judge Larsen sent two young men to prison and put seven others on probation for either twenty-four or thirty-six months. Five of the seven were required to do C.O.-type work for twenty-four months, one for thirty-six months.

Judge Larsen wrote six memoranda in 1970. Two were appealed and affirmed. One was Scott Alarik's non-registration case that I already described.

By far the most interesting memorandum by Judge Larson in 1970 involved James Kerwin, a Carlton College student who filed his completed application for C.O. status fifteen days after his board sent him an induction order. The local board granted Kerwin a courtesy interview to determine the reason for defendant's lateness in filing his claim. Judge Larson found that the local board's examination of the source and substance of defendant's Conscientious Objector status at the courtesy interview amounted to a "reopening in fact" of the classification. The result of the finding by the court of reopening was a cancellation of Kerwin's order to report for induction. Thus the court examined the merits of Kerwin's C.O. claim in spite of the lateness of his claim. Kerwin was found not guilty. Judge Larson relied upon decisions in the district courts of South Dakota and Rhode Island and the Court of Appeals for the Ninth Circuit. *Kerwin* was decided by Judge Larson on April 27, 1970. Less than four months later on August 7, 1970, Judge Larson decided the case of Douglas Ready, a young man just out of high school. Mr. Ready also filed his C.O. application shortly after the local board mailed his notice for induction. He also had a courtesy interview with his local board. The only written account of the events that transpired during a subsequent personal interview with the board indicated that the board asked about Ready's religious beliefs, his church going habits and his parent's religious belief—all issues that went to the source and substance of Ready's C.O. classification request.

Judge Larson found Ready guilty. He distinguished Ready's case from Kerwin's because in *Kerwin* he was left with the "inescapable impression" that the local board decided the case on the substantive merits of Kerwin's C.O. claim. He drew a distinction between "considering" the merits and actually "deciding" on the merits.

In *Ready* Judge Larson wrote: "The court feels that while the defendant's local board may have considered the substantive merits of the defendant's application, that this was not the source for its final determination. In *Kerwin*, Judge Larson stated that the court

> . . . thinks that the critical issue is whether, at such a discretionary interview, the board makes any inquiry whatsoever into the merits of the registrant's claim.

Thus his newfound distinction between *Kerwin* and *Ready* is in direct contradiction to his written memorandum.

Judge Larson then acknowledged that this important distinction was taken from a "recent decision from this same district which was handed down after the *Kerwin* opinion." He was referring to Judge Lord's decision in *Schmidt*.

This new distinction seems to leave the result open to any choice the court cares to make.

An uncharitable independent observer might speculate that Judge Larson's impressions of the process reflect the difference between Kerwin, an articulate Carlton College student and Ready, a young man just out of high school and without substantial verbal or writing skills.

Judge Larson reaffirmed the position he took in *Ready* in October of 1970. John Young filed a late C.O. claim and raised the same issues. Judge Larson found Mr. Young guilty. Judge Larson, who so boldly acquitted Timothy Hansen in 1969 did not acquit another defendant who filed a late C.O. claim during the Vietnam era. In spite of his own sound reasoning and the opinions of other courts he never again found that a local board's action was a "reopening in fact" of a registrant's file.

In 1971 Judge Larson acquitted a defendant who was sent an induction notice on the same day as he made inquiry of the board, the total facts had the look of punitive action by the board, which the court found violated fundamental fairness.

In January of 1972, Jerry Kelley was found guilty. In August of 1972, Phillip Godfrey was found not guilty. Both cases concern a registrant who filed a timely C.O. application; was denied the requested classification; did not appeal the resulting 1-A classification to the board of appeal; refused induction; and was, thereafter, indicted.

In *Kelley* the record showed that the local board failed to consider the defendant's claim and the court so found. Defense counsel argued that this was a violation of due process. Judge Larson did not specifically respond to the due-process argument other than to hold that in his view the U.S. Supreme court decision in the *McGee* case decided on May 17, 1971, precluded "raising this due process claim as a defense." Judge Larson added his own argumentative and highly debatable conclusion that if the defendant had appealed,

> the alleged error of which defendant now claims would clearly had been remedied . . . As in *McGee* the alleged error in the instant case is exactly the type of error which the administrative appeal process is designed to remedy.

On August 10, 1972, Judge Larson acquitted Phillip Godfrey. Mr. Godfrey's draft board, unlike Mr. Kelley's, did meet and consider his C.O. claim but rejected it. In rejecting the claim, the local board did not state the reason for its action.

Judge Larson rejected the government argument that Godfrey, like Kelley, should be precluded from presenting his defense because he failed to appeal. In doing so, he once again set forth the competing rational (1) that the exhaustion doctrine allowed the system to develop a factual record and exercise its expertise and (2) in the absence of a written statement of reasons, appeal within the Selective Service system is virtually meaningless.

Judge Larson concluded that "the only logical conclusion that can be reached is that since the local board's failure to set forth a statement of reasons has rendered the appeal process within Selective Service System virtually meaningless, a registrant should not be precluded from raising as a defense to a criminal prosecution the local board's actions."

The government understandably urged Judge Larson to rely on his decision in *Kelly* and convict Godfrey. To his credit, Judge Larson does not ignore the challenge but his response is less than forthright.

His response was that ". . . in *Kelly* the argument asserted by the defendant in *Godfrey* was not even presented to the Court as a possible defense."

Judge Larson should have re-read his decision in *Kelly*. The defense put forward the very argument that he now accepts. Furthermore, the defense in *Kelly* presented to Judge Larson the decisions and cases that permit review in the absence of exhaustion which lead to the conclusion Judge Larson now reaches in *Godfrey*.

It seems impossible to argue that one's due process rights are less trampled upon when the local board ignores your classification request then when it acts upon your request and fails to state a reason.

Judge Larson would have done well to state clearly that *Kelly* was wrongly decided and to invite *Kelly*'s counsel to move the court for immediate relief from his sentence and discharge of his felony conviction.

On April 4, 1972, Judge Larson acquitted Donahue E. Jones, who I represented. On April 7, 1972, he convicted Robert J. Hruska.

In each case, the defendant had filed a C.O. request that was denied by the local board. In each case, the court discussed the existence of a sufficient statement of reasons.

Donahue Jones refused induction on June 18, 1970. On June 21, 1971, at the request of the U.S. Attorney, four members of defendant's local board met and reviewed the file and supplied the assistant U.S. Attorney with three reasons which they stated the local board had relied upon in denying, defendant's application for C.O. status seventeen months earlier. Judge Larson did not rule on the propriety of this conduct; instead he examined the reasons given and rejected each reason.

The reasons given by the local board were as follows:

1. It appeared the registrant did not set forth sufficient information that his beliefs were acquired through rigorous training.
2. In the opinion of the local board, the registrant's conscientious objection claim does not establish that his beliefs are deeply held.
3. In our opinion the registrant has used expediency as a basis for his claim.

After citing the regulations and case law, Judge Larson disposed of these "reasons" as follows:

There is no requirement of "rigorous training" in the law.

As to the lack of "deeply held" beliefs, a clear requirement of the law "this bald conclusory statement which it refers to as a "reason" is unsupported by any facts cited by the board and the record reveals no such facts that could be cited.

As to the "expediency" claim this is also a proper standard but once again it is a "bald conclusory statement" unsupported by any facts cited by the board or any facts found by the court in the file."

Thus the court acquitted the defendant.

In *Hruska* the local board prepared a short summary after it reviewed Hruska's C.O. application. It contained two words "not sincere."

Judge Larson looked no further. He stated:

This court, therefore, finds that if due process does indeed require a local board to formulate a statement of reasons for denying a conscientious objector application, the statement formulated by the local board in the instant cases satisfies this requirement.

There are differences between the *Jones* case and the *Hruska* case. Mr. Jones appealed to the State Selective Service Appeal Board; Mr. Hruska did not. Judge Larson's decision implied that if one does not appeal to the Selective Service Appeal Board that any "bald conclusory statement" satisfies due process. It is a remarkably denuded concept of due process that one would not have expected of Judge Larson. Mr. Hruska deserved better.

Judge Larson had no hesitancy to reject statements in the registrant's file that were not legally sufficient "reasons." He did so several times, including another case I tried before him in April of 1972 for Timothy Olmscheid. Mr. Olmscheid was teaching in the Virginia, Minnesota, junior high. The school made a strong statement satisfying the criteria for a teaching deferment. The local board thought that Mr. Olmscheid should go into the service and then come back and teach. Judge Larson held that the statement of the local board was not a legally valid reason for denying the teaching deferment. He acquitted Mr. Olmscheid.

A few other cases of Judge Larson are interesting. Quentin Boone was a full-time student and classified IIS (student deferment). He was reclassified 1-A after he dropped out for a quarter. When he returned to college as a full time student he was not reclassified. He received a notice of induction and advised the local board that he was a full-time enrolled student. The board canceled his induction but did not reclassify him II-S. Instead they gave him a temporary classification, I-S(c). Boone did not appeal, although he asked the board once more for a student (II-S) classification. The board classified him IA and made no statement of reasons for their action.

Judge Larson held that the absence of a statement of reasons by the board was a fatal procedural error and following his decision in *Godfrey*, Boone's failure to appeal did not preclude him from raising the defense. He entered a judgment acquitting Mr. Boone.

In 1972 Judge Larson ruled that a denial of a request for a teaching deferment required a statement in the record for the board's action, and in another case involving a teacher he found that the board's statement was not a legally valid reason for denying the requested deferment. In yet another case involving a teaching deferment, he required a statement of reasons even though the registrant did not appeal the denial of his request for a teaching deferment.

He also acquitted James Leavenworth in August of 1973 because the local board sent him a notice to report for induction within the thirty-day period following his classification. This deprived Leavenworth of the full thirty-day period in which to appeal. The board, realized its mistake, sent a second order, and indicted Leavenworth on two counts for not responding to either order. They argued that the second order gave him the full appeal period. Judge Larson noted that there was no reason for anyone, let alone the registrant, to know that in someone's mind the registrant, after receiving the second order to report for induction, could then appeal from the classification made before the first order of induction.

Two decisions by Judge Larson, in November 1973 and May of 1974, were very unfortunate. Both involved a failure to register. Bruce Carlson registered five months late. His indictment and prosecution took place after the last persons were inducted during the Vietnam War. The probability of Carlson being drafted was zero even before he got a high lottery number. Judge Larson permitted Colonel Robert Knight, state Selective Service director to testify that, following the lottery, there was an upsurge in late registration by men who had received high lottery numbers. There was no direct evidence that Boone knew of his obligation earlier. It was offensive to use Colonel Knight's testimony to supply the guilty knowledge that a defendant had a duty to register.

Ronald Boucher registered for the draft seven months late. In both *Carlson* and *Boucher,* the Selective Service testified that they had a publicity program regarding the duty to register. The program consisted of press releases to newspaper and television stations and posters in various locations throughout the states. The only poster in Boucher's hometown of Robbinsdale was located in the second-floor office of the local Selective Service. Boucher's attorney introduced the Selective Service book of the local board that identified the names with date of birth of those persons born in the years specified and records of the dates upon which those persons registered. On the page containing the defendant's name and the two pages before and after that page, forty-seven persons were registered who had completed the registration process later than Boucher.

Judge Larson was unmoved. He repeated the lottery evidence from the *Carlson* case and dismissed the argument of the defense.

Boucher appealed, and his conviction was reversed. The Court of Appeals strongly disagreed with Judge Larson's decision in *Boucher* as well as the decision of Judge Neville on which he relied. It was the Court of Appeals and not Judge Larson who noted that the only local poster was on the second floor of the Selective Service office and, further, that the deputy director of Selective Service could recall only one article on the subject of registration actually appearing in a newspaper. In reversing Judge Larson, the appellate court said:

> No facts exist upon which to draw any inference that Boucher knew of his obligation to register during this period and his actual registration does not give rise to an inference that Boucher knew of the duty to register during the proceeding months.

In reviewing the specific local board registration pages, the appellate court noted that those pages list seventy-six men born in 1954 who registered between March 1973 and April 1974. *All of the men registered late* (a fact also unmentioned by Judge Larson), and forty-seven registered as late or later than the defendant.

The unspoken argument seems to be the most powerful argument. There was a large group of men in the defendant's community and age group who, at the very least, were unclear as to the timing of their obligation to register.

We are indebted to Judge Ross for the following note in dissent.

> One cannot logically ignore the obvious fact that Boucher became eighteen shortly before the end of fighting in Vietnam and did not register until several months after the end of the war and after the announcement that there would be no more inductions under the Selective Service Act.

If the court is to conclude from this "obvious fact" that Boucher and everyone in a position similar to Boucher all have perfect knowledge of these facts and the law, then we must conclude that one hundred percent of Mr. Boucher's contemporaries were willing to risk a felony conviction rather than expose themselves to the possibility of being forced to go to Vietnam or be forced into the U.S. Army. If that were so, I wonder how Judge Ross and those who would agree with him propose to deal with such a circumstance. I would note that the fact that one hundred percent of those reaching age eighteen after the draft ended registered late might well reflect the fact that the end of the draft created the widely held belief that it was no longer necessary to register for the draft. Following the reversal of Mr. Boucher's conviction, the conviction of Mr. Carlson was vacated.

On at least three occasions Judge Larson was faced with a defendant who claimed his due process rights were violated by the Selective Service process in handling appeals or hearings with such brevity that only a few seconds were devoted to each case. Judge Neville had ruled that such a hearing violated due process in a case involving Duane Wallen, and the argument became know in Minnesota as the "Wallen" argument. Judge Larson noted the decision of Judge Neville and expressly criticized it and refused to follow it. Judge Neville noted Judge Larson's views and responded vigorously affirming his position. These cases will all be discussed in the section concerning Judge Neville's decisions.

A more detailed discussion of the decisions of Judge Larson is included in the end notes.

Judge Larson convicted seventy-two percent (fifty of sixty-nine) Selective Service defendants in the contested court trials that came before him in the Vietnam era. That fact standing alone might be explained as an artifact and not a true representation of his judicial activity. But an examination of the decisions shows that his conviction rate was driven by decisions in a number of contested legal areas:

He ruled in one case that a draft board had reopened a file and thus cancelled an induction order, yet refused to adopt the same position in any other case that came before him.

In a case where a registrant failed to appeal to the Board of Appeals, he ruled that due process required a draft board to state its reasons for denying the applicant's request, but he refused to apply the ruling in a case where the local board totally ignored the request.

He looked at the reasons given by the board and submitted them to severe scrutiny to determine if the reasons were mere conclusions as distinguished from facts, and, on at least one occasion, he accepted as a sufficient statement of reasons the words "not sincere."

He found at least two defendants guilty of registering late upon inferences that were not justified by the facts or the law.

He rejected all efforts to raise due-process issues involving the appeal process, although such concerns were real and substantial and resulted in acquittals of defendants in other cases.

We were able to examine Judge Larson's reasoning in thirty-three of the sixty-nine cases he decided. It is fair to conclude that in at least ten and more probably about twenty-four of the cases in which he found a defendant guilty, a different judge might well have found the defendant not guilty.

Chapter Seven

Judge Philip Neville

"Old White Knuckles"
   Judge Neville exhibited great distress and often pounded the bench at sentencing, hence prosecutors referred to him as "old white knuckles."

On January 20, 1972, Dave Gutknecht was indicted after he refused an order to report for C.O. work. He was arraigned before Judge Neville on May 15 where bail was set at $10,000. He refused counsel and asked for an immediate trial before a jury. On June 11th he was found guilty and sentenced to three years. With Dave's permission and the assistance of a law student, Greg Gaut, we brought a motion to reduce Dave's sentence.

In order to support the motion, Greg and I did a study of every case disposed of by the Minnesota district court between January 1 and September 15, 1972. A copy of the affidavit presented to the court at the motion hearing on September is included in the Appendix. The sentences of selective service violators for the first eight and a half months of 1972 were as follows:

2-year prison term	1
1-year prison term	3
6-month prison term plus probation	20
60 days plus probation	1
90 days plus probation	1
Probation plus five	10
Probation or suspended sentence	<u>28</u>
	69

Judge Neville took the motion under advisement.

On October 31, 1972, Judge Neville entered his order. He reduced Gutknecht's sentence to two years.

Two years was still a very long sentence that late in 1972. Indeed Judge Neville himself had not sentenced anyone to over six months in

Dave Gutknecht walking into Minneapolis Induction Center among supporters. (Courtesy of the *Minneapolis Star Tribune*.)

jail in a Selective Service case since 1970 except for the two "Minnesota Eight" defendants. Judge Neville would prove to be the most difficult judge to "judge" on the Minnesota bench and in many ways the most interesting and challenging. It was a pleasure to try a case before him, and he was open to new and creative arguments. The results as set forth in the Appendix are unique. He tried fifty-seven court cases and found twenty-five (forty-four percent) not guilty. From the defendants' point of view, that was a better record by far than anyone except for Judge

Judge Philip Neville.

Lord. On the other hand, including guilty pleas and jury convictions, he sentenced a total of fifty-nine defendants. Of those, he sent an astonishing fifty to jail! Almost all were six-month sentences.

It's important to take a closer look at Dave Gutknecht's case. I had made several arguments for a reduction of his sentence. First, I argued that Gutknecht, by taking his case to the Supreme Court, had performed a tremendous service to society. In fact, thousands of convicted defendants had their sentences or convictions reversed and tens of thousands others had their cases dismissed. That was not hyperbole. The reports of the director of Selective Service noted in their summary to Congress that a massive review of convictions and pending cases were required following the Supreme Court decision in *Gutknecht.*

Second, we argued that the parole board did not grant parole to Selective Service resisters. That argument was supported by an affidavit by Dr. Willard Gaylin, M.D., of the Institute of Society, Ethics, and Life Sciences at the Columbia University Medical School. Dr. Gaylin had written an article on his findings published in *Harpers* magazine and also reported the data in his book, *In Service of Their Country.*

We also presented a community detention plan by "Reach Out Today" in which they agreed to accept and supervise Gutknecht in a manner which would permit him to spend some time helping his family.

Third, we argued that a special problem had developed in Gutknecht's family. His sister was dying of cancer. His mother was spending twenty-four hours a day trying to care for her. They really needed Dave. This also was a matter in which no facts were exaggerated. The prison at Sandstone where Gutknecht was serving his sentence before the argument, noted his excellent conduct in prison and had given him a several-day emergency family leave to help establish home health care.

Lastly, of course, we argued that the sentence was out of line with almost all contemporaneous sentences.

Judge Neville was unimpressed. He referred to my argument as "abrasive." Furthermore, he "resents . . . the attempt of counsel to attach to the court the responsibility for separating defendant from his family." He pointed out that before his incarceration, Gutknecht only worked part time for a janitorial service for $100 a month and "was very involved in a so-called cooperative natural food store at 26th and Bloomington Avenue and estimated his earnings at $75.00 per month."

Judge Neville seemed to base his decision on two matters. First, Gutknecht did not turn himself in upon learning of his reindictment. The U.S. Attorney's office submitted an affidavit that asserted that Gutknecht called the U.S. Attorney's office "on numerous occasions" to see if he had been indicted, yet he failed to appear after a summons was issued. The U.S. Marshall's office filed an affidavit that he had a warrant for his arrest in February 1972 and that he contacted his family and was advised "Dave doesn't want you to know where he is." The Marshall's office claimed they spent "three nights a week" attempting to reach Gutknecht.

Gutknecht did not deny that he did not want to be arrested. He went about his regular business and was arrested at an antiwar gathering on Cedar Avenue just off the West Bank campus of the University of Minnesota.

Judge Neville quoted at length from his decision in early 1972 denying an amendment of his sentence to Craig Jensen in which he quotes from an article by Judge Solomon on Selective Service violators. In Gutknecht's case Judge Neville quoted the following from Judge Solomon:

> One who consistently, continuously and flagrantly has flaunted the Selective Service law and is placed on probation has an effect on other registrants, the extent of which is of course, incapable of exact measurement, many of whom have gone to Vietnam or have faced two years in the military.

Judge Neville was born in Minneapolis on March 5, 1909. He was the son of an editorial writer for the *Minneapolis Journal* one of the predecessor Minneapolis newspapers now part of the *Minneapolis Tribune*. He obtained both his undergraduate degree and law degree at the University of Minnesota. Appointed to the United States District Court in 1967, he died in 1974, serving less than seven years. He began his career just as the Vietnam draft cases started and died as they were winding down. Not much has been written about him. He clerked for the chief justice of the Minnesota Supreme Court, lectured on business law at the University of Minnesota law school, served as president of the Hennepin County and State Bar Association, and was a municipal judge and then U.S. Attorney from 1952 to 1953.

An interview I had with Alan Weinblatt, a former clerk of the judge, provided much of the information I have about Judge Neville. Weinblatt is now a highly regarded practicing attorney in St. Paul. He served in the judge's early years and remained close to the judge during his years on the bench. His comments concerning the judge are noteworthy:

> The Judge's attitudes toward prosecutors was as "foot soldiers on behalf of the government just doing their job . . . it was the job of the judiciary to act as kind of a gatekeeper and to make sure that they did not overstep the boundaries.

> He was a very strong process person. Every case had to be looked at— every detail.

> The government really did have the burden of proof.

> His mind was very compartmentalized. He looked at every issue in detail and would not get beyond the issue before him, i.e., "What are the consequences of a determination on this issue? What box do we then go to?"

> He loved the concept of the law and that love drove him to get down to the "nitty-grittys."

> He was less "result-oriented," than anyone with whom I ever worked.

> He looked at the law as being the "grease and oil of society." That's why he was so "process-oriented"; process was a person's right to be heard.

> Once a decision was made by him or the jury that the individual had violated the law, "there was to be a price. The price was not retribution, but it was a price. That was his job."

> He called sentencing a "function," criminal sentencing was, in his view, the most difficult thing he had to do. But he had to do it. "That was his job."

> He used to cross-exam probation officers as if he were defense council, although he had never defended a case.

One of the U.S. Attorneys whom I interviewed said that U.S. Attorneys used to call Judge Neville "old white knuckles" because at sentencing he would grit his teeth, and he would pound his desk with his knuckles. They believed he was in such internal torture over his sentences. The judge's former clerk agreed, "Absolutely correct. It tore at him, I think."

My interview with Weinblatt provided one additional insight in to the sentencing of Gutknecht by Judge Neville. The judge was "upset with the lack of proper decor." I was not present at Dave Gutknecht's original sentencing on June 30, 1972, but it is certain that Gutknecht's decor would not be considered appropriate. His attitude was not helpful. The court inquired as to his desire to make a statement before sentencing. His response was:

> I don't know. I don't really think it would be worth the trouble. As you know, I do not agree with the whole proceedings and I think you know that, that it is useless . . . and worse than that, to be sending people to prison for this kind of thing . . . I do not have any particular bad feelings toward you, I just think what you are doing is really wrong and really useless.

I had considerable experience with Judge Neville before the Gutknecht sentence reduction argument. I had tried at least nine non-jury Selective Service cases before Judge Neville on the merits before the hearing on September 22, 1972. Those nine cases had resulted in seven not guilty and two guilty decisions.

In addition, I had an interesting jury trial before Judge Neville in 1970, as well as the third and final Minnesota Eight trial in June of 1971.

The Northfield 88

In May, 1970, eighty-eight students from Carlton College and St. Olaf College, both in Northfield, Minnesota, along with a young college professor from Carlton (Paul Wellstone) and the Chaplain of St. Olaf "sat-in" on the steps of the induction center in Minneapolis, Minnesota. Their presence, though peaceful, blocked the entrance to the center. All were arrested and charged with a petty misdemeanor under federal law. The law at that time permitted a non-jury trial before a federal magistrate. Almost all people charged with petty misdemeanors waive their right to be tried by a federal judge. These defendants did not.

I was one of five attorneys who appeared for the defense. The case was assigned to Judge Neville, and we brought a motion before him for a jury trial. There is no constitutional or statutory right to a jury trial for a federal petty offense. We persuaded Judge Neville that he had the discretion to grant our motion. In an eight-page order and memorandum Judge Neville granted our motion after setting out a number of conditions that the defendants all accepted.

Eighty-eight persons were arrested and eighty-eight persons came to trial before U.S. Federal Judge Philip Neville and a jury in the courthouse in Minneapolis on June 8, 1970. Bleachers were erected to seat the defendants. While we have had arrests of larger numbers in Minnesota, both before and after, it remains, at least in the memory of those who should know, the largest mass jury trial in state history. Certainly the largest mass trial in federal court.

The trial was exceptional for bringing none of the problems that you might anticipate from a mass trial of would be "protestors." The most newsworthy events of the trial were the testimony of Donald Fraser, then the Representative from Minneapolis to the United States Congress and Peter R. Linkow. Representative Fraser testified in effect that Congress had passed resolutions withdrawing federal authority to the extent it could but that it was powerless to stop the war. At Representative Fraser's suggestion, we called Linkow who had just left the Nixon administration where he had a White House role dealing with students. Linkow testified that the only real brake on the administrations actions in prosecuting the war was the public opposition. He testified that there were people in the White House whose job it was to monitor all possible sources of information concerning antiwar activity. In effect he said, this action, students sitting down in mass at an induction center, would register on the White House antenna and would be noted.

The heart of the defense case and emotional peak of the trial was the testimony of four defendants selected by the group. Each described in detail the personal beliefs that motivated the action. The commitment to non-violence; the obligation to be involved personally in opposing war and the military; the absence of alternatives; the need to express life and hope; the depth of moral shame; the inadequacy of any lesser act.

I drafted an instruction to the jury that included the first amendment of the United States constitution and asked the court to instruct the jury that they could find the defendants not guilty if they believed they acted in the exercise of their constitutional rights.

The court granted the instruction. The jury found the defendants guilty on June 11, 1970.

Several defendants spoke to the court at sentencing after the judge had indicated his intended sentence. None asked for a "lighter" sentence. Each asked the court to take a personal stand. On the day the jury found the defendants guilty, the United States Congress voted fifty-two to forty-seven against a President Nixon proposal to permit military action in Cambodia.

Judge Neville sentenced each defendant to a fine of thirty-five dollars or five days. Sixty-eight defendants paid the fine. Twenty defendants went to their homes throughout the country and on the expiration of the period provided to pay the fine, they reported to the local U.S. Marshals office to be confined. Several Marshals refused to accept the defendants without an amendment to the commitment order. Judge Neville signed separate orders as necessary in those cases.

I doubt that any other judge in our district would have granted a jury trial and permitted the latitude at trial that was granted.

Judge Neville's Selective Service calendar in 1969 and 1970 was already beginning to burst at the seams.

Judge Neville wrote a memorandum in substantially every case in which he determined the guilt or innocence of a defendant. His memoranda are always detailed factually and met and discussed every issue.

In May of 1969, Brian Nelson, a young Jehovah's Witness who had been denied a C.O. classification appeared before Judge Neville. Judge Neville discussed the file in great detail and found nothing in the file to suggest a basis for the board action in denying the C.O. classification. The U.S. Attorney, Joe Walbern, argued that the defendant had various traffic offenses that in his opinion were sufficient to question his sincerity. Judge Neville pointed out, with I thought admirable restraint, that it is hard to relate traffic offenses to crimes of violence that could be a basis for questioning a conscientious objector's sincerity. Moreover, the information relied on by Mr. Walbern was not in the defendant's file when the board classified him 1-A. The U.S. Attorney made other arguments concerning his alleged conduct that were equally farfetched. I commend to those who want to acquaint themselves in detail with Judge Neville's writing style as well as the sometimes excessive behavior of at least one assistant U.S. Attorney to read *U.S. v. Nelson.*

Judge Neville presided over jury trials and sentenced George Crocker and James Dombroski after they were found guilty. I think that it is fair to say that along with Gutknecht, Crocker and Dombroski were the most visible and publicly recognized representatives of the resistance movement at the time.

George Crocker in the audience showing the peace sign at the Universalist Church, March 5, 1969, while young men sign letters declaring that they refuse to register for the draft. (Photo by Krueger, from the *Minneapolis Star-Tribune* News Negative Collection, courtesy of the Minnesota Historical Society)

George Crocker, an older brother of John who was convicted by Judge Devitt, clearly could have received a C.O. classification. He refused and litigated only the issue of the unconstitutionality of the war. Readers will recall that I introduced George Crocker earlier as the "Uncle Sam" present when Dan Holland refused induction and later "took sanctuary" in the Universalist Church in Minneapolis and led the hundreds present in non-violent passive response to his arrest. He was for many in that period the embodiment of the pacifist resistance movement. On March 18, 1969, Judge Neville sentenced Crocker to four years in prison. He reduced the sentence to three years on May 14, 1970, after being presented with evidence that the average sentence nationwide at that time was three years.

Dombroski was convicted in a jury trial in which he served as his own attorney. Some sense of Dombroski and the difference between him and Crocker can be gleamed from reading the court's memorandum of July 3, 1970, and the appellate decision affirming his conviction. Judge Neville describes Dombroski's pre-induction physical as follows:

> Between 6:30 A.M. and 7:30 A.M. that morning, defendant's name was called, he stepped up, was handed his papers to be used in undergoing and recording the results of his examination and almost immediately set them afire.

Members of the RAP (Resistance Action Project) had "surreptiously or otherwise found their way into the room where the inductees were assembled." The Court of Appeals noted the following information from Dombroski's Selective Service Questionnaire form:

Occupation:	"Professional Revolutionary"
Work:	"Carry out subversive tactics."
Employer:	"Castro, Uncle Ho, Mao and their friends."
Business of Employer:	"Head of the World's Revolutionary Struggle."

Dombroski was charged with destroying government property as well as refusing induction. Judge Neville noted that, at the trial, the court permitted the defendant and a number of witnesses who were at the induction center to testify "far beyond the direct issues of the case and to express

95

their feeling of antipathy toward the Selective Service Law, the Vietnam War, and their moral and philosophical views as to our present form of government and its alleged deficiencies and short comings."

On July 23, 1970, two months after reducing Crocker's sentence to three years, Judge Neville sentenced Dombroski to six months in jail for destroying government records and two years for refusing induction. Thus pacifist George Crocker served the longer sentence.

Three Selective Service cases decided by Judge Neville in 1970 were appealed. One case was reversed. Robert Wright, a young man from Duluth brought a civil suit to prevent his induction on the grounds of fatherhood. The so-called "fatherhood" deferment was made available by regulation to any registrant who advised the board that his wife was pregnant before the board mailed an Order to Report for Induction. The facts were not in dispute. Wright's wife was pregnant. The conception occurred before the board mailed the notice. In the ordinary course there was no way that the Wrights would know she was pregnant, the board was notified as soon as possible.

In a beautifully written decision, Judge Neville ordered the board to reopen the file and classify the defendant III-A (fatherhood).

The government appealed, and no one appeared for Mr. Wright. The case was reversed with little discussion of the detailed reasoning upon which Judge Neville's decision was based. Wright was born on May 4, 1944. The case was reversed on June 10, 1971. Wright was then twenty-seven years old and no longer subject to the draft. It is apparent that he no longer cared about the issue. Whether the result on appeal would have been different if someone had argued in favor of Judge Neville's decision is open to question.

One of the noteworthy cases Judge Neville decided in 1970 involved Duane Wallen, who I represented after he refused induction. Wallen had filed a well-documented application for Conscientious Objector status, which was denied by the local and appeal boards.

Copies of the appeal board minutes revealed that the appeal board meeting began at 9:30 A.M. and lasted two hours. Wallen's case was fifty-eighth on the agenda of a total of 122 cases. Most cases were decided five to zero. Averaging out, total time in studying, deliberating and voting on each case (with no break of any kind) was 59.01 seconds.

Thus if more than fifty-nine seconds were spent on any single file, then less would be spent on others. The clerk testified that she prepared a "summary" of all appeal files that were delivered to each member in advance of the hearing. The summaries were destroyed after the meetings.

Judge Neville wrote:

> It does not require lengthy argument to this court to convince that a fifty-nine-second appeal is not a meaningful appeal proceeding. It is almost a routine "rubber stamp" operation . . . In reality [it is] an appeal to the clerk . . . for he or she is the one who makes the resumé, who selects the matters to be emphasized and who omits what she considers immaterial matter.

After a review of the statute, the relevant laws, and regulations, with particular emphasis on the United States Supreme Court's decision in *Oestereich* and *Breen* striking down the "delinquency" regulations, Judge Neville found that the appeal process as applied in the *Wallen* case violated due process and acquitted Mr. Wallen.

Later that year, Judge Larson convicted John Young who first raised a hardship case, and then after his induction order filed a late C.O. claim. His attorney raised the "Wallen" issue. Judge Larsen noted the meager material in Young's file and concluded, "it was a simple case, a claim which could be fairly disposed of in less than a minute." Although it would not be necessary for his decision, Judge Larson described the appeal procedure and found it reasonable, necessary and appropriate, in effect refusing to follow Judge Neville's reasoning. In November 1970, Judge Larson again rejected the *Wallen* argument in the hardship case of Russell Smith.

In January of 1970, Richard Slettenbough brought a civil action against the Selective Service to enjoin his induction. He had a number of personal problems and was attempting to obtain a hardship deferment. He appeared at his local board and had a ten-minute interview during which time the chairman handed him a note saying they would go over the twenty-two new documents later as they did not have the time to do it then. The board denied the claim. He appealed to the appeal board that denied the claim. Slettenbough's action came before Judge Neville. The evidence upon which Slettenbough based his action for an injunction was that the appeal board gave an average of sixty-five seconds each to his and the other 262 cases heard that evening. The U.S. Attorney presented the same testimony from the same witnesses in *Wallen, Young* and *Slettenbough.* Judge Neville had no trouble granting the injunction because of the "blatantly lawless" manner in which the appeal was handled within the meaning of *Oestereich* and *Breen.*

Judge Neville pointedly rejected Judge Larson's argument. He also added this insight into his own behavior.

> The court, before writing this memorandum opinion, spent nearly one hour just in reading the 103 papers contained in this plaintiff's Selective Service file, and, thereafter, made subsequent references thereto. How a Board of Appeals could consider this file in one minute and four seconds and give it meaningful consideration is beyond the ken of this court.

Just a few days before Judge Neville granted an injunction against the induction of Richard Slettenbough, Judge Larson convicted David Treichler of refusing to submit to induction. In *Treichler,* Judge Larson again rejected Judge Neville's argument concerning the appeal process and noted that *Wallen:*

> . . . ignores the substantial amount of time spent by the appeal board members in reviewing summaries and file materials outside of formal board meetings.

As the attorney who initiated the argument, I have never been advised of any case in which a board member or anyone else testified to the amount of time that any selective service appeal board members spent reviewing material outside of the appeal board meetings. It is singularly inappropriate for the court to speculate in such a manner.

During 1970, Judge Neville proved to be consistent. Brian Solem appeared before him in June with Michael Anderson, a Jehovah's Witness, who refused induction. Solem was one of the most active Selective Service attorneys. Almost all of his clients were Jehovah's Witnesses, or members of other religious groups, who would not perform military service. Anderson had filed a C.O. application, which was turned down by the local and state appeal boards. Neither board stated any reason for their act. Judge Neville acquitted Mr. Anderson and, although the case was straight forward, wrote a five-page scholarly memorandum. Indeed, every case I found resulted in a similar memorandum.

In addition to the cases already referenced, in 1970 Judge Neville found a defendant not guilty because a local board sent him inappropriate forms and instructions and acquitted a defendant who was never shown adverse material in his file and whose file did not contain a statement of reasons for their classification.

While Judge Neville was consistent in requiring the local draft boards to follow their rules and regulations and was open to novel arguments that refected his concern for due process, he never accepted as a defense the "late blooming argument," which would require a draft board to reopen a registrant's file and consider a C.O. claim after an induction order had been sent. He convicted several defendants in cases that raised that issue, but he had no hesitancy in making clear that in those instances, if the registrant was inducted into the armed forces it was a requirement of the law that the C.O. claim be considered by the armed forces.

Judge Neville's decision in the case of Bruce Edward Murray, in which he also refused to change his view on the "late crystallization," is interesting particularly because he recognizes the contrary decisions by at least two Federal Circuit courts, the ambiguity by the Eighth Circuit and his hope that "perhaps soon the United States Supreme Court will speak to the issue." It did so in *Ehlert* (April 1971) and essentially adopted the same position as Judge Neville.

The Kronke-Therriault Trial

Judge Neville began 1971 with the jury trial of Francis Kronke and Michael Therriault, the last of the "Minnesota Eight" defendants. When Kronke and Therriault entered the draft board in Little Falls, Minnesota, near midnight on the evening of July 10, 1970, they left a box of letters in their car. They intended to distribute the letters the next day. The letters explained why they destroyed all the 1-A draft files for the county. The F.B.I. were waiting for them, as they had been at Winona and Alexandria, and, thus, they too actually destroyed nothing. But the defendants had long abandoned any notion that a defense could be mustered along any traditional lines. Kronke was a seminary student and very involved in the work of Pope John XXIII and the proclamation of *Pacem in Terris* by the Catholic Church. He decided to represent himself and make opening and closing statements to the jury. Judge Neville granted Kronke that right. The trial became a combination political-religious contest. I had hoped to call Noam Chompsky, from Cambridge, as our primary witness. Chompsky, in addition to being a world-renowned linguist was a most learned and articulate antiwar speaker and writer. He begged off and sent in his place, Daniel Ellsberg. Mr. Ellsberg, a former intelligence officer with the U.S. Defense Department, showed up with a large old-fashioned, top-opening, leather satchel. He carried the satchel with him; in and out of court all the time. He explained that he had papers from a yet secret Pentagon study, and he wanted to release them to the press at an appropriate opportunity. He was in the Twin Cities for five days before he took the stand. During that period, we often talked about his testimony. On every such occasion he would ask, "Will the judge permit these documents to go into the record and be public?"

I tried unsuccessfully to persuade him that it was very likely. He sat in court while the judge permitted Staughton Lynd and others to testify. Finally he took the stand with the promise that I would not refer to "his papers' unless he brought it up. Over U.S. Attorney Thor Anderson's objection, Ellsberg testified to the significance of acts of civil disobedience in setting government policy. He said the chief argument against sending 206,000 more American soldiers to Vietnam in the spring of 1968 was that "domestic unrest, particularly the draft resistance, would be overwhelming." As a result, Clark Clifford, then Secretary of Defense, decided against it. It was clear from the judge's statements that he did intend to let our testimony in and then instruct the jury that all the defense evidence was irrelevant. But Mr. Ellsberg demurred. He did not agree that our trial would be the best place to "release" his documents.

Mr. Ellsberg left the Twin Cities without revealing publicly the contents of his satchel. Less than two weeks later he delivered the "Pentagon Papers" to the *New York Times*. In addition to the defendants appearing on their own defense, the following defense witnesses testified:

David Gutknecht:	One of the founders of the Twin Cities Draft Information Center, Resister, etc.; and the Defendant whose case would later come before Judge Neville upon re-indictment.
Gordon S. Neilson:	Marine veteran of the Vietnam War;
Robert E. Anderson:	Army veteran of the Vietnam War;
Romeyn Taylor:	Professor of History, University of Minnesota. Specialist in Chinese and Asian History;
Marv Davidov:	Peace activist;
Arthur H. Westing:	Professor of Biology, Windom College, Putney Vermont, Director, American Academy for the Advancement of Sciences study on ecological effects of military uses of herbicides in Vietnam; Professor Westing showed color slides to the jury on the effect of American herbicidal practices on the terrain of South Vietnam. These slides had been presented by the Professor to the full academy at a meeting in Chicago only a few days before being shown in court.
Andrew J. Glass:	Journalist. Congressional correspondent of the *National Journal*, a journal devoted to

	the coverage of public questions and feder-al government issues primarily for use as a research tool by other newspapers, government, and corporations.
Daniel J. Ellsberg:	Senior Research Associate, Center for International Studies, Massachusetts Institute of Technology; for 16 years a researcher and consultant to federal government and participant in decision making or national defense issues;
Staughton Lynd:	Historian and author; specialization in his-tory of non-violence, American radicalism, and draft resistance;
Alan Hooper:	Professor of Genetics and Cell Biology, University of Minnesota.
Mark A. Jasenko:	Director of Religious Education, St. Michael's Parish, Prior Lake, Minnesota; former seminarian;
Alfred Janieke:	Priest, Catholic Radical;
William C. Hunt:	Director, Newman Center, University of Minnesota; priest; attended Vatican II as official expert in theology; Professor of Theology at St. Paul Seminary.

I am not aware of any court in the country where such an array of testimony was presented to a jury. No other judge in our district would have permitted the defendants to present that testimony to a jury.

Judge Neville instructed the jury substantially to the effect that none of the defense evidence was relevant to the issues before them. On January 18, 1971, the jury returned a guilty verdict.

During jury selection, the defendants deliberately left a Vietnam veteran on the jury expressing the view that he had a right to hear the evidence and decide the case. The veteran became the jury foreman. He spoke to the defendants after the verdict was returned and ex-pressed the opinion that the court's instructions left the jury no choice, but he wanted to apologize to the defendants for his personal participa-tion in the war.

The Court of Appeals affirmed the jury verdict on May 30, 1972, and Judge Neville sentenced each of the defendants to five years in prison. On June 7, 1972, Judge Neville denied a motion to reduce the sentences.

Later in 1971, I represented Ralph Crowder, a teaching assistant at the University of Minnesota, who was working toward his Ph.D. His department head sent his local board letters indicating that Crowder was teaching full time. He was denied deferment based on a local board memorandum that "a full-time graduate student shall not be considered for occupational deferment because he is engaged in teaching part-time." Thus, there was a factual dispute as Crowder was allegedly a "full-time" graduate student and a "full-time" teacher. The local board never acted on Crowder's request, only the clerk. Judge Neville found that the request was "not frivolous" and, as a matter of law, the board must rule on the disputed factual issues. He acquitted Mr. Crowder.

Essentially the same legal issue was presented in a different manner in the case of John Trepp. Trepp was classified 1-A and objected on the grounds that his physical exam was inadequate and that they ignored letters and evidence that he suffered from a serious knee disease. He wrote a letter to the board, which objected to the incomplete physical and suggested he would "retake the physical, or see a specialist, or whichever you prefer." He did not specifically use the term "appeal." The clerk put the letter in the file. Judge Neville ruled that the decision as to how to treat the letter, i.e. a possible appeal, at the very least belonged to the board and not the clerk. He acquitted Mr. Trepp.

In another interesting case, James Levin claimed he never received his 1-A classification and, therefore, was denied his right to appeal. The facts are very complex. Levin was registered in Duluth but worked in California. He regularly sent letters to the local board advising them of his address. The Selective Service file showed one address inside the file and another address on the file cover. The clerk "assumed" the right address was used but could not be certain. Levin testified that he never received the 1-A notice. The government made three arguments. First, a defendant cannot raise the question of receipt of his classification notice; second, the law presumed he received his notice; and third, the court cannot look at any facts not in the Selective Service file.

Judge Neville rejected all the government arguments as violative of due process, found reasonable doubt that the notice was correctly sent and acquitted Mr. Levin.

It was a measure of Judge Neville's consistency that he had some doubts about the defendant's conduct but was, nonetheless, committed to the defendant's right to due process of law.

Draft calls for fiscal 1972 (July 1, 1971 through June 30, 1972) were approximately 50,000 nationally, dropping from a high of approximately 290,000 in 1969. The draft ended in January 1973, after a peace treaty was signed between the United States and North Vietnam.

Yet it was during 1972 that the court faced an explosion of Selective Service indictments. The majority of criminal cases in the Federal Courts in Minnesota in 1972 were Selective Service cases. These cases resulted in 148 adjudications and 110 sentences. An additional forty-five persons were sentenced after 1972 before the Vietnam era Selective Service prosecutions ended.

Judge Neville adjudicated eighty-four Selective Service cases during the Vietnam era. Fifty-seven of those cases were resolved in 1972 and thereafter. Thirty-five of those cases were court trials. He acquitted fifteen and found twenty guilty.

Thus, during the entire Vietnam era, Judge Neville sentenced fifty-nine Selective Service defendants to prison, but only six were sentenced to more than six months. Those six were: Five years to the two Minnesota Eight defendants, three years to George Crocker, two years to Dave Gutknecht, two years to James Dombroski, two years to Roger Yule, and one year to Robert Doyscher. Mr. Yule's court trial resulted in an eight-page memorandum detailing Mr. Yule's efforts to avoided being drafted. Mr. Doyscher pled guilty before Judge Neville on April 12, 1972. I was not able to discover anything that would explain Mr. Doyscher's sentence

Judge Neville was the only Minnesota judge to discuss his sentencing attitude in a Selective Service case memorandum. The first case where he wrote about sentencing involved Craig Jensen. Jensen did not file a C.O. application until after he received his induction order. Judge Neville found him guilty, sentenced him to serve six months in prison to be followed by twenty-four months on probation doing C.O.-type employment under the supervision of the probation office for that twenty-four months. By then, this was a typical sentence by Judge Neville. Jensen obtained the required employment before beginning his jail term and brought a motion to reduce his sentence to eliminate the jail term.

Judge Neville denied the motion. He stated that he already gave Jensen the benefit of the doubt that he was a Conscientious Objector. His analysis began by equating the request with asking him to impose a sentence which:

> would be the equivalent of what the draft board would have ordered if he
> had made and established his claim.

Judge Neville set out a number of reasons for his not being prepared, except in some (unspecified) instances, to place such defendants on probation. These are:

1. Congress passed a law and provides a penalty.
2. The Court cannot substitute its judgment for that of Congress.
3. It would weaken law enforcement and the "intendment" of the law.
4. Enforcement must involve some inconvenience and hardship to those who chose not to obey it.

Judge Neville also quoted at some length from an article by Judge Gus J. Solomon of the U.S. District Court for District of Oregon published in May of 1970.

The thrust of Judge Solomon's article, entitled, "Sentences in Selective Service and Income Tax Cases," was that, unlike other laws, Selective Service and income tax laws are dependant upon the cooperation and compliance of the citizenry. The systems (Selective Service and tax) would break down if people did not comply with the law. Thus, the usual considerations of protecting the public, or the need of the defendant for rehabilitation or the need to avoid depreciating the seriousness of the offense do not apply.

Judge Solomon wrote that income tax and selective service violators must be confined "as an instrument of social control."

And Judge Solomon believed that, although tax frauds are morally reprehensible, longer sentences must be imposed on Selective Service violators than on income tax violators. The reason was precisely because many selective service violators "are idealists, with good backgrounds and excellent education. . . . When a person is charged with an income tax violation, mere publicity of the offense is a form of punishment because it produces in the offender a feeling of shame and social disgrace."

For that reason, Judge Solomon believed jail time of sixty to ninety days for the prominent income tax evader was sufficient. "Unlike the usual income tax violator, a Selective Service violator does not experience any feelings of shame or regret. There is no stigma attached to detection and conviction. He will not lose the respect or friendship of his peer group."

In May of 1972, Judge Neville sentenced Ted Dooley. Doug Hall made an impassioned plea to the court not to send Dooley to prison. Judge Neville responded basically that Congress made the law, he took an oath to enforce the law, and that if there was no serious penalty for violating the law, it made a mockery of the law. He continued as follows:

> Maybe it should be repealed, maybe we shouldn't have any draft, maybe we shouldn't have any war, or maybe we shouldn't have any army. But, those are not this Court's decisions, I don't think.
>
> I appreciate your strong feeling about it, and you are not the only one that feels that way; many do.
>
> But, as I sit, I must administer the law as far as I can as a Judge in accordance with what it is, and I can't say to myself, "Well, that is a bad law and, therefore, fellows that don't obey it, it doesn't amount to anything." Because if we start that, then anybody can say he doesn't like the tax law or he doesn't like the drug law or he doesn't like any other law, and he does not obey it because, well, he feels that it should not be the law.

The very theory of a democracy is of course, that we elect our representatives, and they pass laws and those that don't like it still must abide it.

How much of a deterrent a jail term has on others, I don't know. I know that in the last six months, a great number of those that are before me have concluded that they would go into the service. Whether that was because they feel it is an alternative to what they think the Court might do, I have no way of proving, but I think the United States Attorney's records will show that—I am going to say as many as [fifty] percent of the cases before me in the last six or eight months, I may be a little high on that—have elected to go into the service.

Now, maybe you think if the threat of imprisonment forces them to do that, that that is not fair either. But tactically that is what has happened, and I have talked to the other judges, and they have had the same experience.
A good many of those registrants have gone into the service, some of which haven't been accepted, by the way, but I have given a good deal of thought to it. I wrote a little memorandum on it once, and you may have seen it in a case as to what my philosophy should be.

Some courts in this Eighth Circuit mete out, if you look at the statistics, four or five years with regularity. Other Courts take a different view and particularly out West, I think a good many probations. I have tried to adopt a policy that I thought was a fair and as equitable as it could be.

I am sorry that you are so upset, and I realize Mr. Dooley is upset.

Judge Neville sentenced Dooley to six months in prison followed by eighteen months on probation.

In October 1972, Judge Neville's reduced Dave Gutknecht's sentence from three to two years. At that time, he quoted at length from his memorandum in the *Jensen* case, including his quotations from Judge Solomon's article.

The moving papers and Judge Neville's order in Gutknecht's case as well as Judge Solomon's article are reproduced in the Appendix.

Judge Neville does not specifically direct his remarks to opponents of the Selective Service system as opposed to the "ordinary" defendant.

Judge Solomon was not so reticent. He wrote:

I occasionally give probation in other draft cases, but they usually involve special circumstances. If a defendant is not placed on probation, how does one determine the length of sentence that should be imposed? Should all violators get the same amount of time?

Should the ordinary student be given the same sentence as a student body president or the editor of the college newspaper?
What about the young man who doesn't report for induction because he is personally opposed to the war but has never attempted to influence anyone else? Should he be given the same sentence as a militant resister—the young man who makes speeches, passes out leaflets, and marches in parades?

Isn't the militant entitled to exercise his constitutional rights to express his opposition to the war, just like his United States senator, without subjecting himself to additional penalties?
These are difficult problems. I have wrestled with them for a number of years, and I have changed my mind many times. *At present, I believe that since the primary purpose of sentencing Selective Service violators is to deter others, longer sentences should be imposed on those violators who occupy prominent positions in student and antidraft organizations. I intend to impose sentences of two years.*

For the follower, I would impose a sentence of eighteen months or, in the alternative, two years, with the requirement that the defendant spend six months in a jail-type institution and the balance of the time in civilian work of national importance."

I believe it is because of similar attitudes by Judge Neville that George Crocker was sentenced to three years and James Dombroski and Dave Gutknecht to two years. There is no explanation for the longer sentence to Crocker. Originally Crocker received a four-year sentence. Only after hearing motions and receiving evidence that it was the longest sentence for refusing induction in Minnesota did Judge Neville reduce Crocker's sentence to three years. Could it be that Judge Neville believed he had the greatest influence on others? Was it because the members of his family were resisters? Was it because his father was a World War II resister, which fact Judge Neville found both incomprehensible and most abhorrent? I am at a loss to explain or discover a standard that would result in a greater sentence to George

Crocker than to any other person in Minnesota who refused induction or registration during the Vietnam War.

During 1972, Judge Neville made a number of decisions involving errors or unlawful assumptions of power by the local board clerk or the board itself. In early 1972, I represented James Jannetta. He had been deferred as a teacher and subsequently classified 1A and sent an induction order. His induction was postponed at his request. During the postponement, he requested that his file be reopened because he had just been accepted by the Peace Corp to teach in Afghanistan upon an application filed a year earlier. The clerk contacted the state office and advised Mr. Jannetta that there was no authority to reopen his file.

Judge Neville disagreed. The board had an obligation to meet and decide whether or not the facts warranted reopening. Mr. Jannetta was acquitted.

In July of 1973, I represented Donald Erickson, who sent a letter to his local board the day before he was to report for induction. The letter established a good case for a Conscientious Objector classification. The secretary of the board called the state board, and the officers at the state conferred. "They agreed that we should not interfere with the man's reporting."

Judge Neville ruled that it was up to the board to make a determination of the facts and to either reopen or refuse to reopen the file and state the reasons for their action. Judge Neville entered a judgment of acquittal.

A few days after the *Erickson* case, Judge Neville found Michael Dozark not guilty. Dozark filed a C.O. claim after an induction order in June of 1972. The board refused to reopen, and he refused induction. At the trial Dozark produced evidence that he and two other Mankato college students visited with the clerk before returning to college in the fall of 1971. They all testified that the clerk told them that the student deferment was in the process of being abolished but, based upon his lottery number, he (and also another registrant) would not be called until late, probably in November. The clerk did not deny the conversation. Dozark testified that he had planned to file a C.O. application in the summer and was shocked to receive a notice on June 8th.

Judge Neville found the testimony credible and that the defendant had established all of the necessary elements to raise a valid defense. He acquitted Mr. Dozark.

In a series of decisions, Judge Neville examined the basis or reasons for a local board's decision and found them factually and legally insufficient.

Lawrence Leistiko filed a C.O. application that he delivered to the board personally. He had a personal appearance at his request. The board denied his application and wrote: ". . . the board believed Mr. Leistiko's claim was based upon political beliefs and failed to justify the Conscientious Objector claim." He appealed unsuccessfully and later refused induction. The appeal board minutes read "expediency and insincere."

Judge Neville noted that there was nothing in the file that pointed to evidence or objective facts that would constitute the reasons why the local or appeal board reached the conclusion it reached nor was there anything noted in the file that could serve as the basis for those conclusions.

Judge Neville acquitted Mr. Leistiko and commented:

> The line may be thin between the definition of the words "conclusions" and "reasons" but in this case at least the court believes "reasons" were not given but mere "conclusions."

Judge Neville made a similar decision in a case involving somewhat more complex statements by the local board. David Lang was a student at the University of Minnesota and a teacher in rural Wisconsin. At issue were the following statements in the file:

"Lacks evidence of sincerity,"
"Personal beliefs,"
"Expediency,"
"No supporting evidence."

Judge Neville discussed in detail the applicable law and concluded:

> The file must show affirmative evidence of insincerity or bad faith not lack of evidence of sincerity. Clearly defendant views fall within the law and are not "a merely personal code."

> Expediency is an unexplained term and grounds which this court has never deemed one for denial of a request for a classification. It is not clear what the term means in the present frame of reference.

> Form 150 states directly that the *filing of such supporting statements is optional*. The minimal demands of the due process clause of the XIVth Amendment at least require notice to registrants that lack of supporting statements will jeopardize their applications.

> The due process clause does not allow the government to publicly offer a choice and then, sub silento, penalize those who exercise the preferred option.

He acquitted Mr. Lang.

The question of when a statement is a mere conclusion and not a factual reason also arose in James Higbee's case in September 1972. Higbee's case was acknowledged by Judge Neville to be somewhat more difficult simply because the local and appeal board wrote longer statements, but after a full review, he acquitted Mr. Higbee. He adopted the view in the most recent Fourth Circuit decision that the board must state,

> . . . whether it has found the registrant incredible or insincere or of bad faith, and *why*.

One further decision by Judge Neville demonstrates that he took the prosecutors burden of proof seriously. Michael Lewis, a St. Paul resident, asked that his file be transferred to St. Cloud at the time he was ordered to take a physical. He gave an address in St. Cloud and stated, "I am living in this area." A month later, he was ordered to report for induction in March. The letter was sent to his former address in St. Paul. Mr. Lewis did not appear. The clerk then wrote to him in St. Cloud and inquired if he were still a student at St. Cloud State College. A second induction order was sent to both the St. Cloud and the St. Paul addresses by registered mail. Neither was delivered.

I represented Mr. Lewis after he was indicted for two counts of failing to submit to induction. Because of the complexity of the order of induction process the sole question was the validity of the first order to report for induction. The U.S. Attorney produced a number of papers from Lewis' February 1971 physical that showed his St. Paul address and argued that the St. Paul address was the address "last reported to the local board." Thus, they argued, the regulations created a presumption of receipt upon mailing.

A detailed examination of the medical records however did not show a single instance in which Mr. Lewis had written his address as St. Paul or signed his name to a page with that address. The only signature or initials appeared to be those of the examining officials. The form was typed and signed by the clerk, and it was probable that it was filled out by the clerk before the examination. The doctors appeared to have simply copied the typed information they were given.

Judge Neville found the defendant not guilty.

Chapter Eight

Denouncement

In Judge Solomon's view, the need for social control required that draft law violators should almost always be sent to prison and active resisters given the longest sentences. This was not based upon his belief in the ignoble nature of the defendants or the wisdom and righteousness of the Vietnam War.

Not only did he believe that these law-breakers were idealists, the true "Best and Brightest" that America had to offer, he clearly stated his opinions. He believed that Selective Service defendants had been influenced:

> By respected public figures—Senators, Congressmen, and other people who hold high political and military office; by presidents of great and respected universities; by well-known scientists, scholars, writers, and church leaders; all of whom say that our participation in the Vietnam War is unjust, immoral, and illegal. Many of these prominent people also say that the draft laws are unfair, immoral and illegal.

Judge Solomon did not leave his view of the public attitude toward the war in Vietnam in doubt. It was central to his sentencing beliefs. In speaking directly to the need to sentence "as an instrument of social control" he explained his views of the war.

Americans have become unhappy with our participation in the Southeast Asian war. This is particularly true of young people. They are frightened and worried about themselves, their future, and the world in which we live. Their worries are exacerbated by what they hear and see over the radio and television. They are distressed by the poverty and racism in our cities. They are affected by demonstrations on college campuses against the military and for more meaningful participation of young people in their quest for a better and more peaceful world. They are shocked by the horrible pictures of death and destruction in Vietnam.

I am not surprised that so many young men violate the draft laws.

It is precisely because of the situation he describes that he sees the need for prison sentences for draft law violators. And for the same reason he believes that the leaders must be given the most lengthy sentences.

I think Judge Solomon is to be congratulated for setting forth his position with such clarity. It is unfortunate that none of the Minnesota Federal Court Judges did so. Clearly the beliefs expressed by Judge Solomon help explain the behavior of all of the Minnesota justices. But the paucity of comments on the war and explanations for sentences is not my major objection to the actions of the Minnesota judges in sentencing Selective Service defendants.

My objection is to the Judge Solomon paradigm and to the acceptance of this model by our courts. A legal system that punishes a defendant more severely if he acts out of moral conviction rather than to achieve personal benefit or gain is a legal system that does not deserve our blessing or respect. It is one thing to say that moral conviction standing alone is not a defense to a violation of a law, but it is quite another to conclude that acting out of conviction that the law is "unfair, immoral and illegal" deserves a greater punishment than acting to avoid personal penalty or discomfort. Thus, if a defendant acted privately or even secretly to avoid the draft, he was rewarded with a lighter sentence than one who advised the Selective Service personnel of his actual or intended violation of law or acted publicly. Providing a premium to one who violates a law secretly or with purely selfish motives is a strange incentive for any system of law.

114

To some extent every sentence has among its purpose that of "social control." But the model used in these cases punished defendants precisely because the defendant "makes speeches, passes out leaflets, and marches in parades" or "occupy prominent positions in student and antidraft organizations." This is activity fully protected by the First Amendment of the United States Constitution, and it is bilge to claim that the conviction is for activity that is not protected by the First Amendment. Since when has constitutionally protected activity been a reason for enhancing a criminal sentence? And here the particular protected activity is that which is most praised and glorified by all as that activity in which all people, especially young people, are encouraged and cajoled to partake.

And partake they did in record numbers, with the result that in record numbers they were punished.

If the reasons set forth above are not sufficient to move the Judge Solomon sentencing model to the trash bin, then note one additional reason Judge Solomon gives for sentencing Selective Service violations more severely than income tax violators. Judge Solomon would sentence those convicted of income tax fraud to sixty or ninety days in jail. But, in his opinion Selective Service violators must be sentenced to more time in jail because the income tax offender will have a "feeling of shame and social disgrace" while "there is no stigma attached" to convictions for Selective Service violations. "He will not lose the respect or friendship of his peer group. In fact, he probably will be treated as a hero, a man of courage and conscience."

So now we have it. A federal judge is not only duty-bound to follow the law, he is duty-bound to be a cheerleader and take steps to mold public opinion to support the law, or at the least to take public opinion into account in his sentencing. And he takes public opinion into account in a most peculiar way. To the extent that the public opposes the law or believes it is a bad law, his duty is to increase the sanctions for violations. Even as the judge recognizes that the law is wrong and is perceived as wrong by so large a portion of society that violators are heroes, it is his job, that is, his function to do everything he can to take that status into account in sentencing each individual who comes before him.

We should examine this idea carefully. Consider the following case. A man is a member of a firing squad. He is opposed to the death penalty. If he pretends to carry out his assigned duty and instead aims and fires his rifle above the head of the condemned man, even if he is discovered, he will receive a minimal sentence. But if he lays down his rifle in plain view of all and refuses to participate in the execution, then his sentence will be greatly enhanced. And if scholars, educators, politicians and many others from all walks of life oppose the execution and thus applaud his action, then his sentence must be further enhanced. The example could be a lot worse. In the example, the secretive violator also acted out of moral conviction that the execution was wrong. And in the Vietnam era Selective Service violators, many of the non-public violators, believed the war or the draft was morally wrong. But of course many acted to avoid the draft for a multitude of other reasons.

The peculiar absurdity of Judge Solomon's position is exposed by an additional question that leads to others. What sentence would the judge impose if the execution were so widely popular with the public that the defendant who publicly threw down his arms would be berated, spit upon and fired from his employment all because of his unpopular action? Would he then reduce the sentence to little or no jail time? How would the judge measure the reception in the community that the defendant might receive? Would he commission polls? Perhaps overnight tracking polls? Or could we hope that he would give up the effort to determine the public attitude toward the defendant and realize that the ABA's "Standards Relating to Sentencing Alternatives and Procedures" in effect at that time were intended to govern Selective Service cases. Those standards recommend a sentence not involving total confinement is to be preferred in the absence of affirmative reasons to the contrary. As Judge Solomon stated, none of the reasons for confinement set out in the ABA Standards (protect the public from further criminal activity, the need for the defendant to be rehabilitated, and shocking crimes which are morally reprehensible) apply to Selective Service cases.

Judge Neville, expressed his agreement with some of the sentencing conclusions of Judge Solomon. His actions showed that he agreed not only that most draft laws violators should receive jail time, but also that the most active should receive the greatest sentences. Thus the substantial sentences to George Crocker, Gutknecht, and Dombroski. But Judge Neville never indicated that he had adopted that part of Judge Solomon's quoted views relating to leaders or activists. Nor did he express any opinion of his own on the Vietnam War or the facts and attitudes motivating young men to violate the draft laws.

The trials of the college students from Northfield and the last of the "Minnesota Eight" defendants as well as the sentencing of Gutknecht provided Judge Neville with particularly good opportunities to express himself on the war. To the extent that he did express himself, he limited his comments to rulings that the Vietnam War was irrelevant to the proceeding.

There is something seriously wrong with a legal system that brings defendants before it because of the war, determines that the war is irrelevant to the proceeding, and then sentences most harshly those who most strongly make known their opposition to the war.

Judge Neville's strong views on the due process rights of those who came before him resulted in his remarkable record of acquittals. It is possible that at least at some level he recognized the incongruity inherent in the process. That recognition may have fueled his commitment to affording defendants the fullest opportunity to put forward their views and his dedication to due process of law.

Yet whether he did or did not recognize the contradictions and incongruity in the legal system, it did not result in any hesitation in his sentencing. He followed the Solomon paradigm, almost all must go to prison, and the activist-resister must go to prison longer.

117

It is unlikely that Judge Devitt shared Judge Solomon's views on the war. It is quite probable that he supported the war to the bitter end. In most of his cases, Judge Devitt was not a particularly harsh sentencer. Yet, in draft law cases he was indeed harsh. His initial sentences to Pence, Gutknecht, John Crocker, and Terry Petersen as well as his sentences to the "Minnesota 8" were all lengthy. Except for the Minnesota 8, the appellate courts reversed each case on the merits. It is clear from Judge Devitt's decisions and the criticism of those decisions by the appellate courts that Devitt was a strong believer in sentencing for "social control."

An overview of Judge Devitt's actions on draft cases leaves little room for equivocation. He was not a good judge. He had little concern for the complexity of the law, and less for the rights of the defendants before him. The problem Judge Devitt presents is much different than the inquiry into the mind of Judge Neville. It is this:

"How is it that no one ever publicly took exception to Judge Devitt as a 'most distinguished jurist'?"

The high pedestal on which he was placed and kept during his life can be explained in terms of "class" without much disagreement from honest observers. He was the favorite judge of corporations, civil defendants, and prosecutors. His courtroom was always hostile to product liability or personal injury litigation. He expected defendants in criminal cases to throw themselves on the mercy of the court.

This explains his pedestal, but does not explain the absence of a contrary point of view. Surely draft law cases were not the only field in which Judge Devitt was a "bad judge." Newspapers in the Twin Cities carry columnists and are open to a variety of public commentators. Law school professors have both tenure and significant access to the media. In point of fact, public criticism of Judge Lord in the press and elsewhere was common. Why was Judge Lord "fair game" but not Judge Devitt? Judge Lord surely had his faults as a judge, but he was a good lawyer with a good understanding of the judicial system, and he was capable of reaching remarkable heights as a jurist on many occasions.

I do not subscribe to a "conspiracy" theory as an explanation for social phenomena simply because I have no easy answer. I do believe the answer lies with the anthropologists and sociologists. But part of the answer is that it is always easier to criticize those who are perceived as "anti-establishment." It is simply easier to "get along by going along."

As to Judge Larson, the conclusions are most disappointing. He was the intellectual leader of the bench, with a strong history of decisions supporting civil rights, fair employment, and fair housing. It was always a pleasure to be in his courtroom. There can be little question but that he had great concern about the war. A substantial amount of anecdotal material as well as his personal comments when interviewed attests to his skeptical if not hostile attitude toward the war. His wife was reported to have sat in his courtroom to encourage lighter sentences to draft resisters. Judge Larson was close to Senator, later Vice President, Walter Mondale who broke with the administration and expressed his opposition to the war in October 1969.

Nothing he ever did or said in his courtroom reflected anything at all about the war in Vietnam excluding the one case in which the State of Minnesota attempted to enjoin the federal government from sending a Minnesota reservist to Vietnam. In that case he merely held that the questions before him were political and outside the courts "competency."

Judge Larson's sentencing behavior was not fully consistent with Judge Solomon's views. He did not send most of the convicted draft case defendants to jail. Of the seventy-seven defendants he sentenced, he sent thirty-one to jail—a rate slightly less than Judge Devitt but not approaching Judge Neville's rate.

The severity of his sentences, however, as shown by the equivalency scale I've used, does not approach either Judge Devitt or Judge Neville. But when it came to sentencing activists or resisters, he did not differ significantly from the other judges. He did not have before him the active vocal resisters that some of the other judges had, but he did not spare the ones he had. Mark Suchy and John Samborski each plead guilty before Judge Larson in early 1968. He sentenced them both to two years in prison while commending their character. Both were pacifist resisters. He sent Alan Jones, an organizer at the Twin Cities Draft Information Center, to prison for eighteen months in May of 1970. In May of 1971, he sent Scott Alarik to prison for two years. Scott, probably the youngest resister to ever come before the court might well have been found not guilty by a bolder court. Surely Alarik did not deserve a two-year sentence by any moral scale unless one was doggedly committed to Judge Solomon's rule—i.e. the more moral the defendant, the more idealist the defendant, the more likely he was to inspire others to follow him—then the greater should be his sentence. Scott Alarik, high school distributor of an anti-registration booklet, fit the Solomon rule perfectly.

But it was not in the sentencing area that Judge Larson was the most disappointing. He convicted seventy-two percent of the sixty-nine draft violators tried to him as non-jury cases. Only Devitt's seventy-four percent conviction rate exceeded Larson's rate. While he struck out boldly in an early case involving a C.O. application filed after an order to report for induction, he soon backed away from that position. I obtained not guilty decisions from Judge Larson (as I did from Judge Devitt) in a number of interesting cases, e.g., an illegal order issued within thirty days of classification, not cured by a second order; a statement of reasons found to be "bald conclusions" in a C.O. case; a C.O. claim found to be timely and the defendant-teacher entitled to deferment, not postponement of induction. But in the main he was hostile to most defenses. His approval of the Selective Service appeal process was slavish. His readiness to convict late registrants of violating the law without proof that the defendant knew of the obligation to register was unforgivable.

I am at a loss to explain Judge Larson's decision-making during the period. I am sure he truly believed that the decisions he made were "correct."

One of the possible explanations for Judge Larson's decisions is that he was influenced by the existence of the war to "rally around the flag." The United States Federal Courts have a history of acting shamefully during wars. The most notable examples are the cases that permitted the internment of American citizens and non-citizens of Japanese descent during World War II. During World War I the courts did little to stop the harassing of Socialists who opposed the war or persons of German descent. It is clear that many of President Lincoln's acts during the Civil War would not have passed constitutional scrutiny at any other time. Judge Larson's approach to scrutiny of the facts suggests that he had a strong sense of the need to support the military and the government particularly in those situations where an adverse decision might strike at a process that was perceived as fundamental to the draft. This would explain his refusal to set aside the administrative appeal process and his unwillingness to force the government to prove that an eighteen-year old knew that he must register upon reaching his eighteenth birthday.

As to Judge Lord, I have less to say. He sentenced only seven draft defendants to prison and then only three for more than six months. All three of his substantial jail terms were to resisters, i.e., Holland (1970, two years), Pence (1972, one year), and Sagedahl (1970, two years). Holland's conviction was reversed following the *Gutknecht* decision.

Certainly Judge Lord's conduct in suggesting jail time to Pence and Gutknecht before conviction was unjudicial. His admonitions at Holland's sentencing that he would increase Holland's sentence if his supporters did not "behave" was likewise inappropriate.

But the simple explanation that Judge Lord followed the shifting public attitude to the war does not fully explain his behavior.

Judge Lord sentenced fifty-four draft defendants; only the three resisters received substantial prison terms. The only rational explanation was that Judge Lord, like the other Minnesota judges, believed that active resisters should spend some significant time in jail.

David Pence was convicted by a jury before Judge Lord for refusing to do alternative service in March of 1971. He was not sentenced until March of 1972. During that year, Judge Lord publicly agonized over the sentence.

Why should he be in agony? He sentenced forty-seven others to probation without jail. But Pence was different. He was a draft resister. Thus even as late as March 1972, he must be sent to prison. It may be too strong to say that Judge Lord "believed" in that part of Judge Solomon's sentencing justification. It might be better to suggest that he "felt" some compelling need to sentence those who actively opposed the draft.

His decision-making was likewise complicated. Judge Lord and his law clerks stated that they looked for ways to find a defendant not guilty. But Judge Larson reported how carefully he and his clerks read the registrant's file to see if everything was done properly. And clearly Judge Neville scrutinized the records.

Judge Lord wrote at least one very conservative decision in which he severely limited the concept of "re-opening in fact" when a local board reviewed a C.O. claim filed after an order for induction. But he also granted a writ of habeas corpus to my client Harold Hustinga on the grounds that the local board did "re-open in-fact" Hustinga's Selective Service file when they reviewed his late C.O. claim. And the Court of Appeals held that such a re-opening had taken place, rejected the government's appeal, and affirmed the writ.

In most cases Judge Lord wrote no formal memorandum supporting his decision. Thus we are often left to speculate as to his reasoning. That is unfortunate.

To Do Justice

That judges pick from a plethora of rules and theories in an eclectic and arbitrary fashion seems self-evident. What is not self-evident are the various forces acting upon each judge to produce a particular choice. Among the least identified choice is the necessity "to do justice." It often seems that all other choices are considered fair and appropriate—simply following the law. To do justice is to be a maverick—to allegedly act outside the law—even to be lawless. An appeal to justice is somehow thought of as contrasted to an appeal to reason. But there have always been judges who explicitly ground a choice they make on the need for a just result. At one time I thought I might extend this commentary by discussing some of the great judges in our history. I also looked at Federal Judges currently on the bench and found that there is no lack of candidates throughout the country who could be held up as judges who have shown a willingness to take a stand for principle. But on further examination, I discovered that there was no need to look to history or to look elsewhere than within the State of Minnesota at the actions of judges currently on that bench.

In September of 1999 U.S. Judge Paul Magnuson stunned a crowded court room in a highly published case by refusing to accept a plea agreement from Jan Gangelhoff. The defendant was the primary whistle-blower in a University of Minnesota athletic department academic fraud case. In a written statement Judge Magnuson chastised the U.S. attorney's office and grounded his action on his conclusion that the agreement infringed on the defendant's fundamental rights. He invited the defendant's attorney to move to dismiss the indictment. The indictment was dismissed on the prosecutor's motion.

In January of 2001, Judge Magnuson removed himself from the bench rather than comply with an order of the U.S. Circuit Court of Appeals to send a defendant to prison for ten years. It all happened because the defendant had a prior conviction. In 1993 the defendant passed two bad checks for a total of $83.50 and was convicted on a complaint for misdemeanor theft. She was placed on probation for one year. Eight years later, Judge Magnuson accepted her plea in a methamphetamine case and sentenced her to a term in prison of five years and ten months to seven years and two months. Under federal law the minimum sentence was ten years because of the prior misdemeanor and one year probation. If the probation had been one day less, Judge Magnuson's sentence would have been permitted. The U.S. attorney appealed the sentence and insisted on the full ten years. The defendant's attorney attempted to get the misdemeanor charge expunged but the U.S. Attorney objected. Judge Magnuson said that the facts made "ten years imprisonment . . . unconscionable and patently unjust." He wrote:

> The government's relentless pursuit of at least an additional [fifty] months is bewildering, unjustified and petty.

> I am so embittered by the government's merciless conduct that I simply could not be impartial upon resentencing.

In an unrelated drug case, U.S. Federal Judge Michael J. Davis granted a new trial to a defendant on the judge's own motion. The judge's memorandum based the action upon the incompetence of the defendant's attorney. Although the record showed substantial basis for the judge's finding against the high profile defense attorney, insiders stated that the "real basis" for setting aside the jury verdict was that the verdict would have required the court to impose a sentence of eighty-five years. After a new trial was ordered, the defendant plead to a count that permitted a fifteen-year sentence.

All of the Minnesota federal judges, and most federal judges around the country, oppose the present sentencing system. These rules have taken from the judges the right to use discretion in sentencing without the approval of the prosecution. In the past, many have written decisions designed to challenge the system and have been reversed by the appellate courts. No Minnesota federal judge acts in a lawless manner, but, when particularly disturbed by the rules as applied to the case before them, on occasion they do their best within the rules to create exceptions, that is, they act "creatively." The attorneys with whom I spoke described the Minnesota federal judges as generally embittered and feeling powerless. These attorneys are of the opinion that the judges act creatively in far too few cases. They would describe the examples I've set out here as very uncommon but not unique.

Judge Magnuson's removal from the sentencing in the case discussed above reflects the courts profound displeasure with the system as well as his response to the rejection of his effort to reach a reasonable result in the case before him. While I am concerned with the federal courts, the comments of a Minnesota state appellate judge in a recent case directly speaks to and advocates creative decision-making by the trial court. In *State* v. *Prabhudail*, 602 NW 2d 413 (Minn. Ct. App, 1999) the Minnesota Court of Appeals reversed the trial court on a sentencing issue. It appears from the record that the defendant entered a guilty plea to misdemeanor solicitation of prostitution, and, over the prosecutor's objection, the trial court continued the matter for one year for ultimate dismissal. He ordered the defendant to pay $100 costs.

The reason for the continuance for dismissal was to avoid providing grounds for the deportation of the defendant who was a lawful immigrant living in Minnesota with his wife and family.

The Hennepin County Attorney appealed. The Court of Appeals in a one-sentence decision reversed. They held that the trial court has no power to make that disposition without the consent of the prosecution. Judge R.A. Randall dissented. His dissenting opinion can properly be described as "scalding" and "soaring."

He noted that the state is "whining" because there was no formal adjudication of guilt, although the court could have found the defendant guilty and imposed the exact same sentence—a one-year informal probation and $100 in court costs.

It is undisputed that the prosecutor's action could cause the immediate deportation of the defendant, creating in Judge Randall's opinion a "grotesque imbalance" between what the defendant did and the consequence of deportation.

Judge Randall argued that the trial court had ample power under the law to dispose of the case without the prosecutor's consent and that the Court of Appeals had no right or power in this case to review the trial court. Judge Randall viewed the decision as "skewed" and "bizarre" but he saved the best for last.

He noted that the case was now before the trial court anew, not only for sentencing, but also for trial and disposition. Therefore, Judge Randall makes two suggestions for a possible course of action that could be taken by the trial court. It is also an action any judge could take when he finds other courses of action sufficiently repugnant. A court may dismiss a case "in the furtherance of justice." Such an order is not appealable. If there is a full and fair bench trial and a finding of not guilty, that is a final judgment and not appealable.

Expectations

In Robert Cover's 1968 polemic against the American judiciary during the Vietnam War, he asked the questions: "What can the judge do? What ought the judge to do without succumbing to the temptation to exceed his legitimate authority?" and finally: "What can we expect from our judges?"

Few would argue with Cover's reminder that, "The men of the American judiciary have not grown from soil which breeds radicalism." Yet he directs us to Lord Mansfield and Justice Story, who refused to contribute to the strengthening of slavery when there remained any legal argument to provide limits. With that in mind, he suggests that we had a right to ask the Vietnam era judge to insist upon the right to counsel at draft board hearings, a right of access to Selective Service files, a right to unprejudiced tribunal for all Selective Service determinations and a right to confront and cross examine any person who would bring adverse testimony or material. In addition to those due process suggestions, Cover would ask the judges to explore the implications of Nuremberg if not for the positive law of America at least for the notion of the *mens rea* of the accused who has a good-faith belief in the criminality of the war and to re-examine the power of Congress and Executive to draft and kill for undeclared wars.

The tragedy of the Vietnam War did not reach the depths of Nazi Germany nor the pain of our Civil War, but surely the American system was in crisis. "Not since the American Civil War has this country been so threatened by disintegration from within, repression from above, and rebellion from below, "wrote Richard A. Falk in the forward to *Undeclared War and Civil Disobedience. The American System in Crisis,* Lawrence R. Vevel. Professors Falk and Vevel wrote in 1970. Twenty years later, Charles DeBenedetti's *An American Ordeal* was published. He wrote: "The arbitrary, military and political conduct of the War intersected with swirling currents of social and intellectual change to produce a crisis of order and authority unknown in the United States since the Civil War."

The federal court in Minnesota met this crisis and ordeal by doing its best to ignore both the cause and its effect. None of the judges showed the moral and intellectual fiber and resolve that we are entitled to expect from our federal bench during such times. If we hope to receive more from the present bench in their current struggle against draconian mandatory sentencing rules, no one can look for inspiration to the courts of the Vietnam era.

Afterwards

What Became of the Resisters?

David Pence

D avid Pence is the one resister in Minnesota who has changed the most since his pre-prison days. On Memorial Day 1974, seventeen months after he left prison, Pence was arrested for carrying a shotgun in downtown Minneapolis. This was part of his attempt to "overthrow" the Minneapolis gun ordinance. He was devoting much of his time to the development of a male militia.

He argued that it was a mistake to grant women the right to vote. "Giving women the right to vote is a way to take away man's vote." He argued that women should stay home and protect the family. The most unproductive creature of all is this "new career woman." In his view, this violated some rational order.

Pence has not changed much since he was interviewed in 1974. For years he had been in the forefront of opposition to abortion, "woman's lib," gay rights, and gun control. In 1992, 1993, and 1994, Pence wrote articles attacking "AIDS mythology" "liberals" and the "stifling ideologies of feminism and gay liberation." He sees the Democratic Party as some kind of conspiracy against men and the masculine culture.

I ran into Pence at the University of Minnesota Wilson Library. He was researching for his new magazine *City Fathers.* We chatted pleasantly and agreed to meet. He was most accommodating and forthcoming during our subsequent interviews.

Pence ultimately went to medical school, became a radiologist, established a large and successful oncology-radiology practice in Mankato. He claimed that outside the Twin Cities eighty percent of the people in the eight-county area centered in Mankato came to him for radiation treatment.

After eight years in Mankato, he sold his practice to the Mayo Clinic because he wanted to return to Minneapolis, basically to pursue his political agenda.

Speculation about the cause of Pence's dramatic change abound.

Pence said in prison he came back to a religious conception of life. He vigorously denied that he was attacked homosexually or otherwise in prison. He claimed that rumors of such an attack were given as the reason for his present attitude. In fact, neither I nor anyone I spoke to had heard such rumors. Pence did receive a letter in prison from the woman with whom he had lived before beginning his sentence; she told him she was leaving him, forming a new relationship with a woman they knew and that they were forming a new woman's home. If the letter did not cause Pence's remarkable change, it certainly provided a focus for the arguments he put forward after he left prison. Before he went to prison he was close to his sister Ellen. She was very active in the anti-war movement. Ellen and Pence's mother started a shelter for abused women in Brooklyn Park. Later they both moved to Duluth and established a domestic violence shelter there. Ellen Pence is an internationally recognized speaker and leader in promoting programs to prevent domestic abuse and services to the victims of such abuse and on other women's issues. Pence's mother, who was a practicing Catholic when he entered prison, has long since left the church. Pence claims that the movement changed, he did not. He refers to abortion as the "centerpiece" of the movement and relates his opposition to homosexuality to a dispute over the politics of requiring tracing of the sexual partners of HIV positive persons. He favored such a requirement and claims everybody else opposed it.

His magazine *City Fathers* is devoted to "respect for God, manly virtue, and the civic friendships which form the basis of democratic life." The first rule of civic dialogue is: "Thou shalt not take the name of the Lord in vain." Civic virtue is clearly "a corps of men" and *City Fathers* guides the "warrior spirit" of men.

Pence did not seem to be a happy man when I last met him. His wife died suddenly in 1999, and he remarried. He has five children, and has since returned to medical practice.

Dave Gutknecht

One of the pleasures of writing this book was renewing acquaintances with people I had not seen for some time. With the help of Don Olson I reached Dave Gutknecht in Athens, Ohio. I had not seen him since he left prison.

Upon his release from prison, Gutknecht resumed where he left off. He returned to his work in the alternative food industry. He worked in the Twin Cities at the co-op warehouse, at Commonplace Restaurant and other places until he moved to Athens in 1989. His closest sister, Ruth, died in 1972 shortly after the sentence reduction hearing before Judge Neville, his mother died in 1984, and brother Douglas died in 1996, leaving one sister from his immediate family. He had less to hold him in Minnesota. A new love and a chance to live in a new community drew him to Athens, Ohio. That relationship fell apart, and he currently has a home next door to the woman with whom he has been partnered for ten years.

In 1979, a year after being released from prison, he began to publish and edit a trade magazine for the food co-op business. In 1985, he began *Cooperative Grocer*, a successor to the first publication. It's a highly professional bi-monthly glossy magazine featuring editorial comment, news related to cooperative business, articles on staffing, sales systems, membership, resources, earnings, and managing, among other topics. Its sponsorship and reach extends across the nation.

Gutknecht joined the food co-op field during the Vietnam War "as a kind of resistance." He remembers speaking of the need to establish democratic peoples organizations to stop the war economy. "Food connects all people." "Deep, personal, creative, non-competitive business organizations create more democracy." His magazine now serves 300 organizations. "I am doing what I've always done: writing, editing, networking, organizing for a more democratic society." He also has refused to file federal income tax returns since 1968.

Dave Gutknecht.

George Crocker

Bill Tilton and George Crocker, pacifist, Quaker, anti-war "Uncle Sam," are the resisters with whom I've spent the most time in the past twenty years. The largest most contentious political struggle in Minnesota after the Vietnam War days did not take place in the Twin Cities. It took place in rural Minnesota when Cooperative Power Association and United Power Association undertook the construction of a high voltage direct-current electric power transmission line from the mouth of a coal mine in North Dakota to a sub-station near Buffalo, Minnesota, an outlying Minneapolis suburb.

The farmers exploded in opposition, confronting the contractors in the fields and toppling the tall, enormous towers required to carry the line. The National Guard was called up to keep order, and when the local county attorneys refused to prosecute farmers protecting their lands, the state attorney general undertook the prosecutions.

In early January 1978 George Crocker moved from Minneapolis to the heart of the dispute and began the task of organizing political activity to stop the line, build defense of those arrested, and advocate non-violent passive resistance to all who would listen.

Ultimately he became the most respected and followed leader in the battle and the most skilled and knowledgeable.

Crocker helped found and lead the broad-based organization that pulled the diverse people that opposed the power line together, GASP, the General Assembly to Stop the Power line.

The history of these events is described in *Power Line: The First Battle of the Energy Wars,* written by Carlton College Professors Mike Casper and Paul Wellstone.

I began to work closely with Crocker during these years and tried a number of felony cases. Crocker was responsible for organizing all of the support work. There were no convictions.

When the Power Companies undertook an extension of that line to southern Minnesota, Crocker organized a Landowners Association of 132 farmers representing one hundred percent of the landowners whose property was being taken for the line.

I represented the association and its members through four separate district court proceedings, two proceedings before a specially appointed three-judge panel, nine months of administrative hearings, and three separate Supreme Court Appeals.

It was our position that the line was not needed, and Crocker often examined power-line experts at the administrative hearings on conservation proposals and the ability of those proposals to limit the need for building increased electrical energy capacity.

Ultimately we prevailed and the proposed line was never built.

Crocker became an expert in the economics and politics of the electrical utility industry. He founded and still heads the North American Water Office that deals with those issues.

He organized and led a coalition of over twenty environmental groups to oppose the above-ground storage of nuclear waste by Northern States Power Company at its Prairie Island Plant in Red Wing, Minnesota, The Prairie Island Coalition. I worked with the coalition and Crocker during the lengthy administrative hearings and, after I closed my office, the Hamline University School of Law Public Interest Clinic that I directed took over representation of the Prairie Island Coalition.

After the Supreme Court ruled that the storage of nuclear waste in Minnesota required legislative approval, Crocker led the opposition before the legislation.

Crocker lives on the same family farm in Lake Elmo, Minnesota, where he and his brothers were raised. He has remodeled the home in a number of unusual ways to make it energy and conservation friendly.

He has been married for over twenty years to the same woman. They have three children. He is still an active member of his local Friends meeting.

The Minnesota Eight

On February 28, 1970, a coordinated action took place against draft board records in St. Paul and Minneapolis.

Large quantities of files and registration cards were ripped and scattered or piled in heaps in Selective Service headquarters on the fifteenth floor of the Post Office Building in downtown St. Paul, the Ramsey County Office on the seventh floor of the same building, and the Hennepin County office in downtown Minneapolis. "Beaver 55" was written on the walls of the three offices. A statement signed "Beaver 55" explaining the action was distributed to news media. A group calling themselves Beaver 55 destroyed draft records in Indianapolis in October of 1969 and eight persons were arrested there. No connection was ever established between the Indianapolis group and the Minnesota draft board raids, and no one was ever charged for those raids. (See *Minneapolis Tribune* March 3, 1970, "Knight says: Draft Raids May Cause Month Delay.") The *Minnesota Daily* of the same date stated that fifty percent of the draft records were destroyed including records for thirty-four local boards in Hennepin and Ramsey counties. On March 4, 1970, the *Minnesota Daily* quoted state Selective Service director Colonel Robert Knight that loss of files may upset lottery and induction orders of local boards.

While no one took actual responsibility for the destruction of those records, Frank Kronke, Charles Turchick, and Brad Beneke took "moral responsibility." Kronke became a spokesperson for the group. On July 11, 1970, draft raids took place in Winona, Alexandria, and Little Falls, Minnesota. The persons arrested became known as the "Minnesota 8." At Winona, Don Olson, Peter Simmons, and Brad Beneke were arrested. At Alexandria, William Tilton, Clifton Ulen, and Turchick were arrested. At Little Falls, Michael Therriault and Kronke were arrested.

The explanation given by the defendants for the state-wide raids was that the Twin City action might have unfairly impacted non-Twin

City registrants by causing a shift in inductions from the Twin Cities to out-state registrants. Destroying draft records at boards outside the Twin Cities would correct that problem.

I represented all of the eight except Cliff Ulen.

Don Olson, then twenty-six, was among the oldest Minnesota 8 defendants. He grew up in the Seward neighborhood of Minneapolis, one of the poorest working-class areas; was a Barry Goldwater conservative in high school, started at the University of Minnesota in 1961, joined a fraternity and the Conservative Students Club, registered for the draft and signed up for R.O.T.C. (Reserve Officers Training). He described his changing attitudes as gradual. Disgust over conservative reaction to the assassination of Kennedy was a marked turning point. He began to read widely, attend anti-war activities and, in April of 1967, attended a mobilization against the war in Washington. He was in graduate school and had intended to follow a career in International Relations. He heard his fraternity brothers discuss their role in the war—including throwing people in Vietnam out of helicopters and attacking anti-war activists. He gave up his career plans, spent 1967 working for Vietnam Summer, and in the fall helped found the Twin Cities Draft Information Center. He spent all of his time in anti-war, anti-draft activity, reading, studying, and teaching. He turned his draft card in on April 3, 1968, was declared delinquent, and refused induction along with Mike Therriault on January 26, 1970. He became a pacifist and close to a number of Quakers.

In the spring of 1970, Olson had emergency surgery and could not participate in the spring student strike. As summer approached he "seemed more and more compelled to non-violently increase his response" to the war and the draft.

The Winona draft raid was intended to be dedicated to George Crocker. The Appellate Court had affirmed Crocker's conviction in April, and on May 14, 1970, Judge Neville reduced Crocker's sentence to three years.

Although all the Minnesota 8 defendants were sentenced to five years, each served twenty-two to twenty-four months. Olson served his sentence at the prison in Springfield, Missouri. On my visit to him in prison, I found the prison medieval, dark, damp, foul smelling, forbidding. I visited all the Minnesota 8 and many others in prison, Milan, Michigan; El Reno, Oklahoma; Englewood, Colorado. I found Springfield the worst—but Don did not complain then or now. He learned pottery in prison and taught pottery when he was released. Since his release from prison, he has been a central part of the co-op movement, the various activities against nuclear power and a pacifist presence at every activity opposing every military action. But, most of all, Don Olson has been and remains the preeminent person in Minnesota for whom one can come for draft or military counseling and advice. For at least twenty years, he has had tables at high schools

Don Olson, March 2002.

relating to military service issues and is the person at the top of everybody's list when asked where one can get information on any military service related question.

For over twenty years Olson has also hosted a radio show on Minneapolis Community owned and operated radio station KFAI. His program deals with issues of social change, social and economic justice and environmental concerns. He has been on the board of directors for years and is now the president of the board.

Don has a twenty-five-year committed relationship with the same woman. He has supported himself since 1980 by selling books and magazines that are not generally available in most bookstores. The publications mostly concern health and the social issues that occupy his life.

I have never known anyone who is so widely and uniformly esteemed. Don Olson is a learned, intelligent, caring radical who presents himself so gently that it seems impossible for him to have an enemy.

He is also a friend who has been of enormous help to me in writing this book. In addition to sharing his story and his encyclopedic, unbelievably detailed knowledge of events and persons, he has spent days with me at the library searching newspaper microfilm for needed references.

Bill Tilton was arrested at the Alexandria draft board with Chuck Turchick and Cliff Ulen. He was one of the most unlikely persons to become a member of the Minnesota 8. As a former vice-president of the Minnesota Students Association and a spokesperson for many of the actions against the war, he was often seen trying to calm down the activities of those whose actions crossed the line from peaceful to provocative.

Tilton grew up in the Irish, middle class, "Macalaster" neighborhood of St. Paul. His father, a railroad attorney, died when Tilton was young. He attended Catholic schools until he started at the University of Minnesota. His considerable wit and ready smile made him immediately popular. He was smart and articulate, he had the skills and willingness to step into almost any situation and take over. He was the leader in any enterprise that gained his attention.

Tilton's explanation of his participation at Alexandria was straightforward. He thought that destroying draft records was right. "If I supported it, I ought to do it."

His mother, who had gone to school with Judge Devitt's wife, was remarkably supportive. She was de-facto chair of a Minnesota 8 parent's committee that was brought together. Bill served his prison time at Milan, Michigan, and became friends with several other prisoners with whom he remains very close.

After prison Tilton worked briefly as a broadcast engineer and disk jockey for a local radio station. As with his prison experience, he made many acquaintances with media people, many of whom remain his friends. He graduated from the University of Minnesota law school and

Bill Tilton and his daughters (left to right) Jessica, Marissa, and Madeline.

was admitted to practice in 1977. Tilton's successful admission to the bar in spite of his felony conviction attested to his considerable skill in presenting himself before the Board of Bar Examiners. His case served as a precedent nationwide for draft-law violators to obtain admission to the bar.

When Tilton was admitted, he began his practice out of my office. He rapidly established himself as a top trial attorney—especially skilled before a jury. He developed an enormous capacity for sustained work and skill in mastering the complex fields of product liability and malpractice litigation. As he developed his practice, he moved from "having an office" to "sharing expense for his office" to forming a partnership with an old friend, Ron Rosenbaum. Tilton and Rosenbaum and I jointly leased space, and when I closed my office in 1994, the space ascended to Tilton and Rosenbaum.

Over the years, Bill became active in community affairs. He chaired a community neighborhood group. Recently he headed up an effort to establish a competitive Kayak course as part of the rebuilding of the Mississippi River just below the St. Anthony dam in Minneapolis. In between, he has become a world-class white-water rafter, traveling and rafting the wildest rivers in China, Russia, Africa, and Chile. Currently he has replaced rafting with kayaking. Tilton has married, divorced, and is a devoted father to his three daughters.

Tilton is still the best known of the Vietnam-era anti-draft resisters but most have no real knowledge of his actual activities. He remains friends with those of the Minnesota 8 who live in the Twin City area—many of whom meet annually at Tilton's legendary Fourth of July parties. They are legendary because they have been going on for over fifteen years, because they are attended by hundreds of young and old people from every era in his life, and because the parties start early and go on forever.

I have, of course, remained a close friend of Bill Tilton's and use his office whenever I have a need in downtown St. Paul.

Charles "Chuck" Turchick was born and grew up in Minneapolis, the son of a Hebrew schoolteacher, a notoriously low paid position. He is very short with light curly hair, now balding. He was a state-class table-tennis player, a humorous young man with a biting wit. He graduated from the University of Minnesota law school and was permitted to take the bar exam after Tilton had broken down the barriers. Although he had high law grades, he never passed the bar. Turchick is intelligent and bright with an often strange, quirky twist to his thoughts. Perhaps the twist to his mind prevented him from passing the bar.

He has worked for several community organizations from time to time and is occasionally seen at meetings involving community or justice interests.

A few years ago he was featured in an advertisement for blackjack at the Mystic Lake Casino in Shakopee, Minnesota, and, shortly after they ran the ad, he was booted out of the casino as a professional card-counter. In fact, he did then, and does now, make his living as a gambler in various local and Las Vegas casinos.

Brad Beneke, like Tilton, is the son of an attorney. His father served many years as county attorney for McLeod County, Minnesota, just west of Minneapolis. He was county attorney when Brad was arrested. Brad's mother was chair of the local Republican Party Club. At the time of the trial, Brad's brother Bruce Beneke had just been discharged from the service. Bruce, an attorney, observed the trial. Shortly afterwards Bruce Beneke became the director of the Southern Minnesota Legal Services organization, the publicly funded organization serving Ramsey County and southern Minnesota. He has served in that capacity for twenty-five years and has built it into one of the premier legal services organizations in the nation.

Brad is thin, wiry and athletic looking. I've often had the feeling that Brad would "spring" into action at any moment.

141

Brad has attempted to get involved in politics supporting candidates but is not particularly involved in social change. He makes his living in the computer industry. Brad is almost always at Tilton's parties and I see him occasionally.

Frank Kronke was working as a program person at the Newman Center on the University of Minnesota campus when he became a spokesperson for the Beaver 55 and then one of the Minnesota 8. I recall him telling the jury during his trial about various members of his family who were Catholic leaders, brethren, or nuns. He had attended Catholic schools and seminary and spoke to the jury at this trial about his Catholic training. His family home was in Southern Minnesota where he grew up.

Kronke left Minnesota almost immediately after he got out of prison. He kept in touch with Daniel Ellsberg, who had testified at his trial, and attempted to write a book about the trial. He sent me an outline, and we spoke, but I heard nothing further. The next time we were in touch, he had been selling encyclopedias. Neither I nor anyone with whom I've talked has been in touch with Kronke for years.

Mike Therriault was born and raised in Minneapolis. His mother was a waitress and seemed ill at ease with the parents of the other Minnesota 8. Mike was quiet and reserved almost to the point of being non-communicative. I felt that Mike shared with his mother the sense that he did not completely fit with the more glib and aggressive group. Mike and Don Olson see each other regularly. Don says that Mike is more political now than he was in the past. He reads more and has worked in food co-ops and co-op warehouses for years. He keeps himself in good physical shape—bicycles everywhere. Mike deliberately keeps his income below the level where he has to file income tax returns. He is a "gleaner," that is, he salvages thrown-away items for use or money.

Peter Simmons was the youngest of the Minnesota 8—only nineteen at the time. He lived with his mother in the Minneapolis suburb of Brooklyn Center. Simmons' mother was a public school librarian and the only parent of a Minnesota 8 defendant who had personally been actively opposing the war. Simmons seemed older than his years and very intellectually inclined. His mother was the most distraught of the parents. She blamed herself for Peter's involvement, as she surely did not want Peter to go in the army.

Peter lives in the Seward neighborhood of Minneapolis and works as a station clerk at Hennepin County hospital. He does not participate in political activities.

Although I visited Peter in prison and kept in touch with him and his mother, I have not heard from either of them since shortly after he left prison.

Others

Fran Shor. The Supreme Court decision in *Gutknecht* required a reversal of his conviction. He was never reindicted. He resumed his studies at the University of Minnesota and obtained a Ph.D. from the American Studies Department. Currently teaching at Wayne State in Detroit, Michigan, he maintains contact with friends from Minneapolis from the anti-war days. He visits here from time to time.

Fran Galt. Galt returned to the University of Minnesota after serving his sentence at the Federal Prison in Springfield, Missouri. He obtained his degree in English. He is currently director of technical services at the Main Library in downtown St. Paul. His father now has a parish in Alabama. Galt does not believe he has changed any of his basic beliefs. He is still a pacifist and a supporter of the Fellowship for Reconciliation.

Fran Galt and Margot Galt.

Scott Alarik. Alarik was a folk singer at high-school gatherings when he was convicted and sent to prison. He took up folk singing seriously in Minneapolis when he returned from prison. Shortly after he moved to the Boston area. He has made his living as a folk singer and publisher of a related magazine ever since.

Brian Coyle. After Brian Coyle's reindictment for failing to take a pre-induction physical was dismissed by Judge Lord, he lived and worked in the Phillips and Cedar-Riverside area neighborhoods on the southern edge of downtown Minneapolis. By 1983 he was working for the Minneapolis tenant's union and became a highly visible community organizer. He was elected to the Minneapolis City Council in 1983 and was its vice-chairman when he died in August of 1991 of AIDS-related complications. One of the first openly gay elected officials in the state, he was eulogized for a lifetime of work on behalf of gay rights, housing for the poor, neighborhood issues and progressive causes. An estimated thousand people attended his emotional funeral. His pallbearers included many state and local luminaries including the mayors of both cities.

Jim Dombroski. After prison he returned to his home in St. Cloud. He moved to upstate New York and was very early into sales of cell phones. He returned to his counter-culture lifestyle but has not been particularly political.

Dan Holland. Moved to Milwaukee where he manages his son's band. He and Don Olson visit from time to time.

Endnotes

Introduction

The bibliography for this book is only a small part of the writings on the Vietnam War. For a more comprehensive bibliography, see *After Vietnam*, John Hopkins Press (2000) and the *Vietnam War and Postmodernity*, University of Massachusetts Press (1999).

Among the books that I found most useful in addition to those mentioned in the Introduction are *An American Ordeal: The Anti-War Movement of the Vietnam Era*, Charles DeBenedetti, Syracuse University Press (1990) and *Working-Class War American Combat Soldiers and Vietnam*, Christian G. Appy, University of Carolina Press (1993).

The references to general draft law violation numbers are taken from *Chance and Circumstance* referred to in the text. Federal Court statistics are all from my study.

Judge Solomon's article on sentencing in selective service cases is discussed in the text and included in the appendix.

A full discussion of Mr. Justice Holmes view of the law and justice is discussed in *Law Without Values: The life, work, and legacy of Justice Holmes*, Albert W. Alschuler, University of Chicago Press

(2000). Most authorities place Justice Holmes on a high pedestal. Professor Alschuler presents a different viewpoint to which I subscribe. He desribes the judicial philosophy of Justice Holmes as follows:

- truth (epistemolgy) is "the majority view of the nation which can lick all others"
- rights (jurisprudence) are "what a given crowd will fight for"
- personal ethics is "in the resort a man rightly prefers his own interest to that of his neighbors"
- a might makes right philosophy

Robert Covers book review can be found at 68 *Columbia Law Review* 1003 (1968).

Author's Note

An excellent discussion of the challenges at home presented after the September 11th, 2001, attacks appears in *The Nation*, November 19, 2001 - "Which America Will We Be Now" by Bill Moyers.

A detailed discussion of the civil rights concerns since September 11th appears in the *Los Angeles Times* of March 10, 2002, under the head "A Changed America - Civil Liberties Take Back Seat to Safety" by Henry Weinstein and Mitchell Landsberg.

A report on the criticism of the war by Daschle and Trent Lott's remarks are in the *New York Times* story reprinted in the *Minneapolis Star Tribune* on March 1, 2002.

Discussions of the proposed defense budget and the quotation from Lawrence Korb is in the *Nation* of March 11, 2002, and *In These Times* for March 18, 2002.

The material covering the new nuclear policy is from the report called "The Nuclear Review" posted on the Internet site by Global Security.org on March 14, 2002, and discussed in an Associate Press article in the *Minneapolis Star Tribune* of March 15, 2002.

The military personnel projections and other material relating to the proposed military assault on Iraq is from an article by Seymour M. Hersh entitled "The Debate Within, the Obiective Is Clear - Topple Sadam, But How?" The article and the sources of the data appear in the *New Yorker* magazine of March 11, 2002.

Chapter One
Resisters Meet the Court

David Pence
Pp. 1-3
Minneapolis Tribune 9/15/74
Interview with Pence 10/4/99
David Harris - *Dreams Die Hard*, Harris, St. Martin Press (1983).
Minneapolis Tribune
> December 19, 1967, "6 Minnesotans Face Draft for Card
> Offences."
> January 6, 1968, "3 State Draft Protestors Receive Induction
> Notices."
> January 23, 1968, "War Draft Foe Refuses to be Inducted."
> March 2, 1968. "Grand Jury Indicts 2 Draft Resister" by Bob
> Lundegaard (Pence & Gutkneckt)

U.S. v. Pence 287 F. Supp. 598,4-68 Crim 21 (Judge Devitt) - Reversed.
410 F.2d. 557 (8th Cir. 1969); 4-70 Crim 157 (Judge Lord)

Dave Gutknecht
Pp. 3-4
U.S. v. David Earl Gutknecht 4-68 Crim 22 (Judge Devitt) 283 F. Supp.
945 (D. Minn. 1968) Affirmed 406 F.2d 494 (8th Cir. 1969), Reversed
396 U.S. 295 (1970); 2-72 Crim 17 - Judge Neville.
Interview with Gutknecht January 7, 2000

Minneapolis Tribune
>January 21, 1968, "Center Offers Advice on Avoiding Draft-3 'Resisters' Man Office." Features -Picture and story about Dave Gutknecht, Sandy Wikenson, and Tom Smit.

Francis Shor
Pp. 4-6
U.S. v. Shor 4-68 Crim 83 (Judge Larson)
Interview with Shor 1/7/2000
Minneapolis Tribune
>January 16, 1968, "'Clean Cut' Protester Refuses Induction" sub head "'U'student (Shor) opposes draft"
>September 14, 1968, "Student is Indicted for Draft Refusal" (Shor)
>April 4, 1968, "9 Draft Cards Turned in at Rally." By-line Molly Ivins.

The Bondhus Family
P. 7
Minneapolis Tribune.
>February 25, 1966, "FBI charges Youth Damaged U.S. Files" - Anti Draft Action Claimed. (Barry Bondhus)
>November 30, 1966, "Man's Trial Opens in Draft Board Defiling." "Big Lake Father of 10 Declares War on U.S. - In draft Case."
>December 3, 1966, "Man Convicted of Obstructing Draft."

Fran Galt
Pp. 7-11
Interview with Fran Galt. January 4,2000.
>On June 11, 1970, the *Minneapolis Star Tribune* featured a picture of Fran Galt his wife and eight-month-old son Jacob under the head

"Draft Resister Recounts Prison Life." The sub-head of the story made reference to a $3,000 grant from the Book-of-the-Month Club for a series of short sketches Galt wrote on black men he knew in prison. Galt currently lives in St. Paul with his family. He is the head of technical services for the St. Paul Library system.

Opposition to the War Grows

Pp. 8-11

The initial buildup of American Forces began slowly. Initially American Forces were limited to military advisors. In 1961 American Forces reached 4,000 and by 1963, troop strength grew to 15,000. In August 1964, following an alleged attack on United States Navy ships in the Gulf, Congress passed the Gulf of Tonkin Resolution, and forces grew to 23,000. In February 1965, the United States began bombing raids and President Johnson increased American troop strength to 125,000. By April 1969, American troop strength in Vietnam reached a high of 543,400. Gradual withdrawal reduced the forces to 23,000 American troops on January 27, 1973, when a peace treaty was signed. See *New York Times,* May 1, 1975, - Stanley Karnow, *Vietnam: A History* (New York: Viking). John S. Bowman, ed. *The Vietnam War: An Almanac* (New York: World Almanac Publications 1985). See also Appendix to Donald L Simmons: *I Refuse* (The Broken Rifle Press, Trenton, New Jersey).

Minneapolis Star Tribune

      March 26, 1966, "Rally Denounces War Involvement"

      March 27, 1966, "City Marchers Are For, Against War."

      June 10, 1966, "65 From State Sign Petition Assailing U.S. Role in War." August 3, 1966. "Pacifist at "u" Arrested; He Won't Fight." (Galt)

      August 7, 1966, "200 War Protesters March from University to State Capitol."

      March 7, 1967, "Draft Charges Stir Debate Among Youths." (By-line Dave Mona)

August 25, 1967, "DFL Dissenters Organize to Fight Vietnam
Policy."

August 14, 1967, "Vigil Planned for Sentencing of Pacifist."
Robert Gilliam, 22, Winona plead guilty before Judge
Larson. (By- line Bob Lundegaard.)

August 15, 1967, "Pacifist Gets 2 Years for Refusing Draft."
"Sympathetic Judge Imposes Sentence." Picture, cap
tion: "Pickets Gathered Outside the Federal Courts
Building Yesterday."

January 6, 1968, "3 State Draft Protesters Receive Induction
Notices, Francis Shor, David Gutknecht, and David
Pence."

January 16, 1968, "Clean-Cut Protester Refuses Induction."
Francis Shor.

January 21, 1968, "Center Offers Advice on Avoiding Draft." "3
'Resisters' Man Office"

March 5, 1968, "2 Young Men, Indicted for Draft Evasion,
Jailed."

Reports of Director of Selective Service for periods ending December
31, 1967, June 30, 1968, and December 31, 1968.

For most of 1968, individual draft violations were "news."
Before the year was up, most reports were of much larger activities.

Minneauolis Tribune: Feb. 9, 1968 - "Rhodes Scholar Returns Draft
Card; Now lA"

April 4, 1968, "9 Draft Cards Turned In At Rally" April 12,
1968 - "Judge Says He Can't Overrule Board" (J. Lord-
Def. Rolf Kolden) This will be the only selective service
decision by J. Lord that is overruled by a higher court.

July 11, 1968, "Group Fails To Get Arrested By F.B.I." "Draft
Resistance Supported." - "300 Persons Rally in City for
Dr. Spock."

July 18, 1968, "Induction Bars Anny Induction of Bemidji
Man." (Judge Harry Blackman, then on the 8th Cir.

Court of Appeals enjoined the induction of Rolf
Kolden.)

August 7, 1968, "17 Turn In Draft Cards At Rally" Sept. 4, 1968
"Youth Given Sentence For Draft Refusal" (J. Larson
sentenced Mark Suchy to 2 years.)

September 22, 1968, "Business of Draft Protest is Booming."

September 24, 1968, "St. Cloud Men Cite Bible, Give Draft
Board Ransom: "Cheered by Crowd, Protester Waits,
Army-Style to Resist." (Dan Holland)

October 4, 1968, "U.S. Dismisses Charge Against Draft
Objector." (Seth Peterson)

October 8, 1968, "War Protester 33, Father of 3 Gets Induction
Notice." (Sid Walter)

October 15, 1968, "Macalaster Won't Report to Draft Boards."

October 16, 1968, "Draft Resister Arrested; Took Refuge in
Church." (George Crocker) "Youth Wouldn't Ask
Objector Status."

October 17, 1968, "MCLU Offers To Provide Attorney For
Draft Resister."

Nov. 15, 1968, "39 Turn In Draft Cards in City Rite."

Minneapolis Tribune

February 9, 1968. "Rhodes Scholar Returns Draft Card; Now
1A."

April 7, 1968, "9 Draft Cards Turned in at Rally."

April 12, 1968, "Judge Says He Can't Overrule Board."

*Rolf Kolden v. Selective Service Local Board No.4. Beltrami County -
Minnesota.* 406 F.2d. 631 (8th Cir 1969) 397 U.S. 47 (1970) [Pending
the appeal to the 8th Circuit and the appeal to the U.S. Supreme
Court]. Kolden's induction was enjoined by the action of Judge Harry
Blackmun. Blackmun was then a Judge of the 8th Circuit and later was
elevated to the United States Supreme Court.

Minneapolis Tribune

July 11, 1968, "300 Persons in City for Dr. Spock." August 7,

1968. "17 Turn in Draft Cards at Rally."
September 22, 1968, "Business of Draft Protest is Booming."
September 24, 1968, "St. Cloud Men Cite Bible Give Draft Board 'Ransom.'"

Holland-Crocker
Pp. 11-13
U.S. v. George Crocker -3-68 Crim 51, 294 F. Supp. 776, aff. 420 F.2d 307 (8th Cir. 1970)
U.S. v. John Crocker -3-69 Crim 87, 308 F. Supp. 998, aff. in part, reversed in part 435 F.2d 601 (8th Cir. 1971).
September 24, 1968, "Cheered by Crowd, Protester Waits Army Style to Resist." "Caledonia Student Refuses Draft." [Daniel Holland was the student (4-69 Crim 47).] Originally sentenced to two years—his case was remanded to the trial court and conviction vacated following Gutkneckt's reversal in January of 1970.

Sydney Walter
P. 12.
October 8, 1968, "War Protester 33 Father of 3 Gets Induction Notice"
November 15, 1968, "From 'U' to Mall, Back Again Hiked the 400." (Byline by MoIly Ivins.

Resistance to Draft Continues
Pp. 10-16.
November 15, 1968. "Dog Burning Doesn't Come Off."
November 15, 1968. "39 Turn in Draft Cards in City Rite."
Minneapolis Tribune
February 14, 1969, "Draft Class Meets Despite Court Ruling."
February 21, 1969, "Students of Draft Are Undisturbed a Second Time."
February 26, 1969, "School Board Votes to Allow Draft Class Sessions to Continue."

March 6, 1969, "16 Say They Won't Register for the Draft." "At
Church Service."

March 12, 1969, "Major's Daughter Fights the Draft."

March 19, 1969, "Court Sentences Resister to Four Years."

April 12, 1969, "Rhodes Scholar From Chisholm Faces Draft."

May 29, 1969, "Draft Information Worker Refuses to be
Inducted."

June 19, 1969, "Police Quell Anti-war Protest in City."

July 12, 1969, "Youth Arrested at Draft Center."

October 12, 1969-October 15, 1969, Many different articles;
"Rally Draws About 10,000 Downtown."

St. Paul Pioneer Press. October 16, 1969.

Bond v. James "Sloppy" Floyd. 385 U.S. 116 (1966).

While the appeal to Supreme Court was pending, the Governor
of Georgia declared the seat vacant and a special election was held. Bond
won overwhelmingly. He then sought the seat again in the regular 1966
election, won the Democratic primary and an overwhelming majority in
the election of November 8, 1966. He later won election to the United
States House of Representatives where he served for 13 years.

U.S. v. Alarik, 4-69-097, 439 F.2d. 1349. (8th Cir. 1971). The
author represented Alarik at time at trial and on appeal, and part of the
facts are from personal knowledge and files. *Minneapolis Tribune,*
December 11, 1969 "Renner Outlines His Draft 'Case Problems.'"

The Gulf of Tonkin resolution was passed by Congress in
August 1964 and served as the basis for the widening war in Vietnam. It
is now widely recognized as based upon a fraudulent claim of unprovoked attack upon United States Navy vessels in international waters in
the Gulf. No unprovoked attack took place. The significance of this
resolution is set forth in the forward by Richard Falk to Lawrence
Velvel's *Undeclared War and Civil Disobedience: The American
System in Crisis.* That book was sponsored by the Lawyers Committee
on American Policy toward Vietnam, University Press of Cambridge,
Mass., The Dunellian Company (1970).

For a more detailed version of the actual events and manipulations that resulted in the 1964 resolution see *Unquestioned Obedience to the President* by Leon Friedman and Burt Neubome. W.W. Norton & Company. 1972. A detailed discussion of 1969 antiwar activities nationwide can be found in *Who Spoke Up: American Protest Against the War in Vietnam*, Nancy Zaroulis and Gerald Sullivan, Doubleday and Company (1994) especially chapters entitled "1969: The Vietnam Moratorium Day" and "1969: Mobilization 'Give Peace a Chance"; *An American Ordeal: The Anti-War Movement of the Vietnam Era.* Charles DeBenedetti. Syracuse University Press (1990); *Hell No, We Won't Go! Resisting the Draft During the Vietnam War.* Viking-Penguin Press. (1991).

Minneapolis Tribune:

> Jan. 20, 1970, "42 Draft Violation Indictments Handed Down.
> May 10, 1970, "Antiwar March Draws 20,000 to State Capital. Demonstration is Peaceful."
> May 13, 1970, "An Historic Minnesota Antiwar March."
> May 20, 1970, "90 Pillsbury Workers Form Antiwar Unit."
> March 4, 1971, "Leaders in DFL Back War Bills."
> March 12, 1971, "Minnesotans Lobby for Peace."
> March 17, 1971, "Vets Support Antiwar Bill."
> April 17, 1971, "St. Cloud Council Asks Vietnam Pullout."
> April 10, 1971, "Minnesota War Tax Resistance Group."
> May 5, 1971, "Fargo, Moorhead Vote for End of Vietnam War." July 1, 1971, "H.H.H., Mondale Hail Decision."
> October 9, 1971, "MFT to Seek Class Discussion of War."
> October 13, 1971, "War Protest Planned for Today in State Cities."
> May 7, 1972, "State's Draft Prosecution Rate One of the Highest." This article by staff writer Bob Lundegaard begins as follows: "Minnesota has one of the highest rates if not the highest—of draft prosecutions in the nation. He quotes Robert Knight as describing himself as an

"aggressive bastard." For the 12 months ending June 30, 1991, Minnesota began 139 draft prosecutions which Lundegaard reports as the same for the states of New York, Connecticut, and Vermont with a populate six times that of Minnesota. Lundegaard also notes, "The recent practice of arresting draft refusers within days of their refusal, rather than waiting for Grand Jury indictments."

Chapter Two
The Draft

Pp. 23-29.

    The source of most of the material in this chapter is referenced in the text. The sources set forth here provide a more detailed history of the draft and its breakdown during the Vietnam War. The specific statement on p. 28 that "By 1972 130.72 legal conscientious objector classifications would be granted for every 100 person inducted" is based on official published data and set forth in Table 7 p. 93 of Stephen Kohn's *History of American Draft Law Violators* entitled *Jailed for Peace.* Stephen Kohn's book also details the July 1863 race riots that broke out in New York City following the publication of the names of local draftees for the Civil War.

- *The Draft 1940-1973* George Q. Flynn, University of Kansas, 1993
- *Little Groups of Neighbors: The Selective Service System,* James W. Davis, Jr., and Kenneth M. Dolbeare, Markham Publishing Company, 1968.
- *Chance and Circumstance: The Draft, the War and the Vietnam Generation,* Lawrence M. Baskir and William A. Strauss, Vintage Books, A Division of Random House, 1978.
- *Jailed for Peace: The History of American Draft Law Violators, 1658-1986,* Stephen M. Kohn, Greenwood Press, 1986.

- *Bitter Greetings: The scandal of the Military Draft,* Jean Carper, Grosman Press, 1967
- *Let's End the Draft Mess,* George Walton Davik, McKay Company, 1967 - *Wrong Man in Uniform,* Bruce Chapman, Trident Press, 1967.
- *Pursuit of Equity: Who Should Serve* (Marshall Commission), 1967, Commissioners Report Executive Order 11299, 1967.
- Annual Report of Director of Selective Service for the Fiscal Year 1967 (July 1966 through June 1967), US Government Printing Office, January 1968.
- Semi-Annual Report of Director of Selective Service for the Period July 1 to December 31, 1967, US Government Printing Office, January 1968.
- Semi-Annual Report of Director of Selective Service for the Period July 1 to January 1 to June 30, 1968, US Government Printing Office, July 1968.
- Semi-Annual Report of Director of Selective Service for the Period July 1 to July 1 to December 30, 1968, US Government Printing Office, January 1969.
- Semi-Annual Report of Director of Selective Service for the Period July 1 to January 1 to June 30, 1969, US Government Printing Office, July 15, 1970.
- Semi-Annual Report of Director of Selective Service for the Period July 1 to January 1 to June 30, 1970, US Government Printing Office, October 1970.
- Semi-Annual Report of Director of Selective Service for the Period July 1 to July 1 to December 31, 1970, US Government Printing Office, March 1971.
- Semi-Annual Report of Director of Selective Service for the Period July 1 to January 1 to June 30, 1970, US Government Printing Office.
- Semi-Annual Report of Director of Selective Service for the Period July 1 to July 1 to December 31, 1970, US Government Printing Office, March 1971.

Chapter Three
Judging

Pp. 31-32.

The terms "memoranda" and "opinions" are interchangeable and are often referred to as "memorandum-opinions." Court rules require "findings of fact" and "conclusions of law" to support a trial court decision or order for judgement but do not require a memorandum.

The case-by-case and paper-by-paper examination of files makes it unlikely that I have recovered every memorandum. In one case the docket sheet indicated a memorandum that I was unable to locate; in another case I located a memorandum in a personal file which was not found in the court file.

The criteria used by West to determine which memorandum-opinions they will publish is not at all clear. It is apparent that they ordinarily only become aware of a memorandum if it is brought to their attention, usually by the judge or one of the attorneys sending a copy with a note suggesting publication.

Chapter Four
Judge Miles Lord

Pp. 33-34.
Minutes of Proceeding. March 5, 1968 -*U.S. v. Pence* 4-68 Crim 21, U.S.C. Gutknecht 4-68 Crim 22.
Minneapolis Tribune.

March 6, 1968, "Judge Gives 2 Protesters Prison 'Taste.'"
March 16, 1968. "Jail Preview for Two Attacked."
Marched 22, 1968, "Judge Reassigns Cases of Two Draft
    Protesters."

In an interview with Judge Lord in July of 1999, Judge Lord acknowledged the accuracy of the news reports.

In Minnesota on June 30, 1972, out of a total of 390 criminal cases pending, 235 were selective service violations. During the fiscal year ending June 30, 1972, out of a total 726 cases, 387 were Selective Service cases. See U.S. Courts Administrative Office Annual Reports of fiscal year ending June 30, 1972. Also Report entitled "Federal Offenders in the District Court."

The author was in court in 1972 and heard Judge Lord's "invitation" to Selective Service defendants. The author was also reminded of the announcement by a former law clerk of Judge Lord. Judge Lord in an interview with the author on July 20, 1999, had no doubt that he had made that announcement. The judge also expressed surprise that he had convicted eighteen. "I didn't think I convicted that many." Although he stated that he always opposed the war, he also agreed that he changed during the war.

P. 35.

St. Paul Pioneer Press.

> March 1, 1972, "Judge Lord Rebuked for Pretrial Remark."
> May 3, 1973, "OEO Chastised by Judge Lord."
> April 4, 1974, "Lord Refuses to Stay Order."
> April 22, 1974, "Lord No Stranger to Disputes."
> April 23, 1974, "That Lord."
> May 17, 1974, "Judge Lord Criticized in Reserve Case."
> November 17, 1974, "Parent Firms Make Lord Bias Change."
> December 26, 1974, "U.S. Judge Lord Voted Minnesota's Top 1974 News maker."
> July 18, 1981, "Miles Lord Gets Award As Top Judge."
> May 20, 1985, "Judge Lord Leaving Bench." "Marvel or meddler, he always 'tried to do right.'"
> May 20, 1985, "A History of Controversy."
> May 20, 1985, "Friends, Critics Say They'll Miss Lord."
> August 27, 1985, "Retirement Dinner Honors Lord."
> September 28, 1985, "Minnesota's Lord Lionized in Dalkon Shield Saga."

December 10, 1989, Byline Don Boxmeyer. "Still the
Maverick/Miles Lord formed his reputation as an
eccentric, feisty Federal Judge. He has retired the
Robes, But Controversy Still Clings to Him."
December 28, 1989, Editorial, "Voice in the Wilderness."
Minneapolis Star Tribune.
January 30, 1993. "If only the Nation had a lot more Federal
Judges like Miles Lord." Source: Peter N. Thompson.
St. Paul Pioneer Press.
May 1, 1994, "Lord's Justice—To Some, Miles Lord is a hero, a
defender of the downtrodden. To others, he is an
ambulance-chasing self-promoter. Now at age 74, he
takes a reflective look back on his career, his family, his
childhood, and his calling."
Acting Attorney General, United States Bureau of Prisons,
Director Norman Carlson. 5-73 Civil 130.
P. 36.
Lord's Justice—One Man's Battle to Expose the Deadly Dalkon Shield.
Sheldon Englemayer and Robert Wagman. Anchor
Press/Doubleday.
Federal Courts - Video - Interview with Miles Lord.

Judge Lord also presided over a habeas proceeding I brought involving Milo Goings, which was very unusual and generated some publicity because Mr. Goings was in transit to the Minnesota Federal Prison in Sandstone when the writ was served. Goings was taken off a federal prison transport bus in Southern Minnesota and sent back to South Dakota. When faced with a second writ to produce Goings, he was tranferred to Levenworth. Judge Lord ordered Clarence Butler, the Assistant Director of the U.S. Prisons who ordered the transfers to appear before him along with Mr. Goings. Judge Lord ordered Butler to transfer Goings back to Sandstone. After a short recess, the U.S. Attorney advised the Court that Norman Carlson, the Director of Prisons for the United States Government had taken away Butler's authority to assign Goings to any prison. Judge Lord released Goings to me, and we left the courtroom.

CBS Channel 4 did an editorial on the next evening about the "Comings and Goings of Milo Goings." They suggested a song title, "Where has Milo Goings Gone." After detailing the facts, they concluded, ". . . now that he's free, he ought to be a lot easier to find."

United States District Court for the District of Minnesota, Fifth Division. *United States of America ex rel Warfield Milo Goings vs. R.L. Aaron, Warden, Federal Correctional Institution, Sandstone, Minnesota*, George Tennennyson, United States Marshall for the District of South Dakota, Robert Bork, United States Acting Attorney General, United States Bureau of Prisons, Director Norman Carlson. 5073 Civil 130.

The Legal papers and files of Kenneth Tilsen including pleadings transcripts, etc.

Minneapolis Tribune.

> March 10, 1973, Picture: United Press International-Caption: "Webster Poor Bear, 22, and Milo Goings, 27, recuperating from gunshot wounds they said they received from federal Marshals while on sentry duty at Wounded Knee Thursday."
>
> November 15, 1973, "Judge Lord Orders U.S. Put Goings in His Court."
>
> November 16, 1973, "Judge Schedules Hearing on Authority Over Prisoner."
>
> November 27, 1973, "Judge Says U.S. Has Mishandled Indian Defendant."

Transcript-Channel 4-C.B.S. November 27, 1973, "Milo Goings' Comings and Goings."

Minneapolis Tribune. November 28, 1973, Associated Press Picture. "Goings Released from Custody."

The Author served as legal director for the Wounded Knee Defense Committee which organized the defense of over 185 federal indictments arising out of the events at Wounded Knee in February through April 1973. The most widely covered trial arising out of that confrontation was the trial of Russell Means and Dennis Banks in Federal Court in St. Paul beginning in January 1974 and ending with a dismissal for government misconduct nine months later. The trial team included national renown attorney William Kuntler, along with Minneapolis attorneys Douglas Hall and Larry Leventhal and the author. The Minnesota Historical Society has a large collection of Wounded Knee material. Among the best of the many books dealing with the events and trials are John Sayer: *Ghost Dancing the Law.* Harvard University Press (1997) and Peter Mathison: *The Spirit of Crazy Horse.* Viking Press (1980).

Pp. 36-37

United States District Court for the District of Minnesota, Fifth Division. *United States of America ex rel Arthur Burghardt Banks v. L.R. Putnam. Warden. Federal Correctional Institution. Sandstone. Minnesota.* 5-74 Civil 9. The legal papers and files of Kenneth Tilsen relating to Arthur Banks. 413 F.2d. 435

TH 72 CR 47 -Southern District of Indiana.

Arthur Banks was released on bail of $1,OOO.OO. The United States attempted to prevent Judge Lord by acting and obtained a writ of Mandamus from the Court of Appeals for the 8th Cir. The writ was denied by a panel of the court - File No. 74-1220.

After extensive hearings, Judge Lord released Banks from further custody on October 24, 1974. The United States appealed. The appeal was dismissed in January of 1995.

After our initial appearance the case was handled primarily by Morton Stavis of Newark, New Jersey. Mr. Stavis, now deceased, was one of the founders of the Center for Constitutional Rights in New York and one of the truly great civil liberty attorneys in all of America.

Pp. 37-38. *U.S. v. Hawley*, 310 F. Supp. 929 (D. Minn. May 26, 1969).

Pp. 38-39. *U.S. v. Schmidt*, 313 F. Supp. 456 (D. Minn. June 3, 1970).

P. 38. *U.S. v. Seager*, 380 U.S. 163 (1965).

"Basis in Fact" is the legal term of art which defines the scope of review of decisions the Selective Service and the federal courts. Like most terms of art it often obscures and confuses. Simply put it means that upon review of a Selective Service criminal conviction the court has a right and obligation to determine if the classification of a registrant, if not in accord with the registrant's request, is based upon facts in the registrant's selective service file.

P. 39. *U.S. v. Kerwin*, 313 F. Supp 781 (D. Minn. May 27, 1970).

P. 40. *U.S. v. Unnach*, 1-70 Crim 10, July 9, 1970.

P. 40. *U.S. v. Coyle*, 4-70 Crim 59, December 7, 1970 (Lord); 6-69 Crim 92 (Devitt).

P. 43. *U.S. v. Gonyer*, 4-71 Crim 125, July 7, 1972.

P. 43. *U.S. v. Ilse*, 5-72 Crim 5, October 31, 1972.

P. 44. *U.S. v. Ball*, 1-72 Crim 60, October 12, 1972.

U. S. v. Pence, 4-68 Crim 21

U.S. v. Gutkneckt, 4-68 Crim 22

It should be noted that the U.S. Supreme Court later decided against the "late crystallization theory." *Elhert v. U.S.*, 402 U.S. 99 (1971) In rejecting post-induction reopening for "late blooming C.O.s" the court established an absolute right of such inductees to obtain "in service" determination of such claims.

Pp. 41-42. *U.S. v. Holland*, 4-69 Crim 47, January 13, 1970 *U.S. v. Young*, 4-70 Crim 31, April 20, 1970.

P. 42. *U.S. v. Sagedahl*, 4-70 Crim 21, April 26, 1970.

Judge Lord initially sentenced Stadler to two years but reduced the sentence while the appeal was pending. The appeal was then dismissed. I tried the Mayotte Trial. It was uneventful.

P. 42. *Minnesota Daily*. January 13, 1970. "TCDIC Advisor Sentenced for Refusing Draft Induction."

P. 42. *U.S. v. Pence*, 4-70 Crim 157. Pence was found guilty on March 23, 1971 and sentenced to a year and a day on March 21, 1972. Other Decisions by Judge Lord:

P. 44. *U.S. v. Gonyer*, 4-71 Crim 125, July 20, 1972.

P. 44. *U.S. v. Isle,* 5-72 Crim 5, November 2, 1972.

P. 44. *U.S. v. Sahlen,* 4-72 Crim 12, January 23, 1973.

P. 44. *U.S. v. Ball,* 1-72 Crim 12, October 12, 1972.

U.S. v. Newman, 4-69 Crim 13, January 31, 1969.

U.S. v. Mayotte, 2-70 Crim 13, March 27, 1970.

U.S. v. Gudmestad, 4-70 Crim 81, November 5, 1970.

U.S. v. Stadler, 3-69 Crim 99, July 13, 1970.

U.S. v. Steams, 4-71 Crim 020 (1971—sentenced 2 months).

U.S. v. Slettehaug, 4-70 Crim 147 (1971—sentenced 6 months).

U.S. v. Beystrom, 5-70 Crim 20, July 30, 1971 (another not guilty decision for Larry Leventhal).

U.S. v. Nelson, 5-71 Crim 133, January 27, 1972. *U.S. v. Lindfors,* 4-71 Crim 341, June 6, 1972.

Chapter Five
Judge Edward Devitt

P. 47. Interview with David Pence October 4, 1999.

P. 47. 4-68 Crim 21 Judge Devitt Memo. 287 F. Supp. 598, July 31, 1968.

P. 47. *Minneapolis Tribune.* 3/12/68 "Lawyer Moves to Quash Charge of Draft Dodging"

P. 47. *Minneapolis Tribune.* 4/26/68 "Court Says It Can't Review Draft Status."

P. 48. *Estep v. United States* 327 U.S. 114 (1946)

P. 48. *United States v. Pence* 410 F. 2d. 557 (8th Cir. 1969)

P. 48. *U.S. v. Pence,* 4-70 Crim 157. Pence Interview

P. 49. *Minneapolis Tribune.* March 11, 1969, "Enemy of Draft Feels Patriotic." By-line story about David Pence by Molly Ivins.

Minneapolis Tribune. March 24, 1971. "Anti-War Leader Convicted by Jury on Draft Charges."

P. 50. *U.S. v. David Earl Gutkneckt* 4-60 Crim 22 283 F. Supp. 945 (May 9, 1968).

Interview with Gutknecht January 13, 2000.

P. 50. Seth Peterson, 4-68 Crim 57 P. 40 Francis Shor, 4-68 Crim 83

P. 50. John Sherman, 4-68 Crim 84

P. 50. *Rolf Kolden v. Selective Service Local Board No.4. Beltrami County.* Minnesota.

P. 51. *U.S. v. O'Brien* 391 U.S. 367 (1968)

Pp. 51-52. *U.S. v. Oestereich* 393 U.S. 233 (1968)

P. 52. Mike Tiger is also the attorney Judge Hoffman had U.S. Marshals arrest at the beginning of the Chicago trial arising out of the 1968 Democratic Party Convention disorders. Tiger was an expert on the law of wiretapping and argued a pretrial motion claiming illegal government wiretapping on behalf of all defendants. Charles Geary who represented defendant Bobby Seale had emergency surgery on the eve of the trial. When Geary could not appear for trial, Judge Hoffman had Tiger brought to Chicago under arrest. The appellate court released Tiger but in the meantime Hoffman had the protesting defendent Seale tied to his chair with the mouth taped. The trial went down from there.

Pp. 51-52. *U.S. v. Gutkneckt* 396 U.S. 295 (1970).

P. 51. *Federal Jury Practice and Procedure,* Devitt and Blackmun. West Publishing Co.

St. Paul Pioneer Press Dispatch:

>March 3, 1968, "Judge Devitt-The Readon Report."
>November 21, 1968. "Devitt Sees Fair Trial Gains."
>January 25, 1969. "Fair Trial Free Press Gains Encouraging, Judge Devitt Says."
>May 1, 1969, "Devitt Lauds Bar 'Peace' Gains."
>July 21, 1970, "Judge Devitt St. Louis Prof Write Book."
>October 17, 1970, "Minnesota 8 Backers Say Judge Unfair."
>June 30, 1971, "6-Man Jury Idea Spreads, Devitt Reveals."
>Some measure of the news coverage of Judge Devitt can be gathered from the following:
>June 8, 1971, "Grads Old Lawyers Needed."
>January 31, 1973, "Devitt Urges Adding Another Judge to State Judicial Unit."

May 2, 1973, "Law Day Speakers Urge Communication."

June 22, 1973, "Supreme Court's Approval of 6-Member Juries Hailed."

September 7, 1973, "Civil Cases Without Juries Proposed."

December 30, 1973, "Service Distinguishes 15."

February 16, 1974, "Religious Town Hall Will Honor Judge Devitt."

April 22, 1974, "Judicial Changes Proposed."

May 22, 1981, "States Federal Judges Disclose Financial Worth."

November 11, 1981, "Citizen Jury Said to Be Outmoded by Judge Devitt."

May 4, 1981, "Judge Devitt to Get Brotherhood Award."

April 15, 1981, "Judge Devitt Appointed."

May 3, 1981, "Judge Devitt Takes Retirement—But He Won't Think of Quitting."

October 20, 1985, "How Local VIPs Made the Grade."

May 2, 1991, "The Judges Judge/U.S. Court Takes a Short Recess to Celebrate a Birthday."

February 22, 1992, "Judge Devitt Being Treated for Brain Tumor."

February 23, 1992, "Veteran Jurist Edward Devitt Calmly Awaits His Final Judgment."

March 3, 1992, "Giant Among Federal Judges/Edward Devitt, Noted St. Paul Jurist Dies of Cancer at 80."

March 4, 1992, "Two Who Graced City from Bench, Street were Gone-Edward J. Devitt Model Public Servant."

March 6, 1992, "Devitt Funeral Sentimental Affair for His Friends-Family and Friends Remember Judge Devitt."

March 5, 1995, "West Publishing Treated Justice to Lavish Trips/Ethics Expert Questions Practice, Paper Says. Devitt Award is Prestigious—And Unusual—Close Involvement of Corporate Sponsor Sets it Apart."

St. Paul Pioneer Press and Dispatch. Pictures and stories concerning Judge Devitt at Award or Christmas Parties or Misc. events include:

> December 21, 1969
> September 21, 1970
> December 15, 1971
> December 17, 1971
> December 21, 1972
> September 19, 1973
> December 18, 1973
> December 26, 1981

P. 55. *U.S. v. Matt Hoffman* 1-71 Crim 100 - September 29, 1971. Brother of Judge Devitt's son-in-law.

Matt Hoffman was a very thoughtful and serious young man who walked into his draft board, received his file from the clerk and walked out of the office file in hand. He deposited it in the trash barrel on the street outside the draft board office. He was originally charged with a misdemeanor but refused to plead guilty. He did not want counsel and although I met with him and his father on several occasions he was determined to be non-cooperative with the court. The case was assigned to U.S. District Court Judge Daniel Thomas of Mobile, Alabama. The newspaper described his case as follows: "Two young grandchildren of federal judge Edward J. Devitt looked on from the front row of the courtroom Tuesday as their twenty-one-year-old uncle was convicted of trying to interfere with the Selective Service System Among the spectators was Judge Devitt's daughter, Terry. She is married to Hoffman's brother."

St. Paul Pioneer Press. September 22, 1972.

Hoffman made a brief statement to the court and then walked out of the courtroom. He was stopped at the elevators and placed in custody when he would not promise to stay in court. He was sentenced to two years and sent to the federal prison in Milan, Michigan. I corresponded with Hoffman and visited him at Milan. With his permission, I filed a motion to reduce his sentence—had correspondence and oral argument with the court in Alabama and ultimately his sentence was reduced to eighteen months.

Minneapolis Tribune. February 12, 1970. "8 Arrests in Draft Raids Spur City Demonstrations. 14 Seized in Protest at Courthouse." [a close reading of the article will reveal that my son David Tilsen was arrested while sitting on a bench in the courthouse waiting for me while I was talking to the arrestees in the jail. The charge was dismissed by the court who lectured the city police on the nature of a public building.]

P. 56. *Minneapolis Tribune.* July 14, 1970. "Stolen Draft Record Found in St. Paul."

P. 56. *Minneapolis Tribune.* July 17, 1970. "F.B.I. Tells of Stakeouts in Draft Raid Hearing."

P. 56. *U.S. v. Beneke. Olson and Simmons* 1-70 Crim 92 and *U.S. v. Turchick. Tilton and Ulin* 6-70 Crim 119 were assigned to Judge Devitt. *U.S. v. Kronke and Thereault* 5-70 Crim-19 was assigned to Judge Neville.

P. 55. Personal material re: Minnesota 8

P. 56. The Minnesota Historical Society has a large collection of Wounded Knee files. Access by permission of the author or others are permitted.

P. 56. *U.S. v. Beneke. Simmons and Olsen,* 1-70 Crim 092

P. 56 *U.S. v. Turchick and Tilton,* 6-70 Crim 119

There were three jury trials before Judge Devitt as the first Beneke, et al., trial resulted in a mistrial.

P. 58. *U. S. v. Coyle* 6-69 Crim 92 - Dismissed January 28, 1970 *U.S. v. Malmager,* 6-69 Crim 54, (Jury trial), March 16, 1970

Pp. 58-59 *U.S. v. Crocker,* 3-69 Crim 87, 308 F. Supp. 998, February 11, 1970. The John Crocker case occasioned remarkable testimony. Mulford Sibley, University of Minnesota professor of philosophy and political science and author and lecturer on Quaker history and beliefs testified directly to the issue as did many others.

Pp. 59-60. *U.S. v. Peterson,* 3-69 Crim 9, March 23, 1970 The Lee case was affirmed without a formal opinion (per curium).

P. 60. *U.S. v. Terrane D. Peterson,* 3-69 Crim 009, July 1, 1971, reversed 456 F.2d 1099 (8th Cir.).

P. 61. *U.S. v. Olmscheid,* 350 F. Stipp. 889,4-71 Crim 253 (April 20, 1972). I represented Mr. Olmscheid before Judge Larson.

P. 61. *U.S. v. Karl E. Burton,* 3-71 Crim 131 (1972), Reversed 472 F.2d. 757 (8th Cir. 1973). Judge Devitt did not write any memoranda-opinion in either *Peterson* or *Burton.*

P. 62. *U.S. v. James E. Roda,* 339 F. Stipp. 182,3-71 Crim 171 (March 8, 1972).

P. 63. *U.S. v. Babcock,* 339 F. Supp. 1281,2-72 Crim15 (April 5, 1972).

P. 63. *Fein v. Selective Service System,* 405 U.S. 365 (1972).

P. 63. *Oestereich v. Selective Service System Local Board,* 393 U.S. 233 (1968)

P. 63. *Clark v. Gabriel,* 393 U.S. 256 (1969).

P. 63. *Breen v. Selective Service Local Board, 396* U.S. 460 (1970).

P. 64. *U.S. Huntsiger,* 343 F. Stipp. 223, 6-72 Crim 124 (June 2, 1972).

P. 64. *U.S. v. Kiemele,* 343 F. Supp. 1300, 1-72 Crim 52 (June 21, 1972).

P. 64. *U.S. v. Jeffery G. Johnson,* 6-72 Crim 103 (May 30, 1972).

P. 64. *U.S. v. Stanley E. Willet,* 4-72 Crim 122 (December 1, 1972).

Other Decisions by Judge Devitt may be found at: *U.S. v. Seeverts,* 1-69 Crim 16, December 22, 1969 *U.S. v. St. Jacques,* 3-69 Crim 46, December 12, 1969 *U.S. v. Lee,* 3-70 Crim 22, July 13, 1970,437 F.2d 897 (8th Cir. 1971) *U.S. v. Robinson,* 3-71 Crim 184,337 F.Supp. 639 (February 9, 1973) *U.S. v. Jerry A. Shaefer,* 338 F. Supp. 371, 2-72 Crim 16 (March 17, 1972) *U.S. ex rel. Bergdoll Drum,* 107 F.2d 897 (rd Cir 1937) *Fishgold v. Sullivan Drydock & ReQair Com,* 154 F.2d 785, (rd Cir. 1946) *U.S. v. Bremicker,* 3-72 Crim 79 (August 16, 1972) *U.S. v. Block,* 3-72 Crim 85 (January 3, 1973) *U.S. v. Burham J. Philbrook,* 337 F. Supp. 70, 3-71 Cr. 181 (February 10, 1972). *U.S. v. Keirn,* 339 F.Supp. 169, 271 Crim 195 (March 14, 1972).

Chapter Six
Judge Earl Larson

P. 67. *U.S. v. Alrick* 4-69 Crim 097 aff. 439 F. 2d 1349 (8th Cir. 1971)

Pp. 67-68. *Minneapolis Tribune:* December 11, 1969 "Renner outlines his draft 'case problems.'" The case was tried to the court with out a jury. Thus the testimony on the motion was the trial testi-mony.

P. 69. *U.S. v. Crocker* 308 F. Supp. 998 (D. Minn.) Aff. in part— reversed in part 435 F. 2d 601 (8th Cir. 1971.)

P. 70. Hennepin Lawyer - May - June - 1979

The Five Ages of Larson by Leonard E. Linquist.

Clerk of Federal Court -video interview of Judge Larson.

Earl Larson - *Commemorative Book* - March, 1993 - Edited Cheryl W. Heilman and Mathew B. Seltzer with forward by Supreme Court Justice Harry B. Blackmum. This book was put out as part of Judge Larson's taking senior status in 1993 and lists the following important litigation: -

- National Football League - free agency approved, Mackey case.

- Minneapolis school desegregation.

- Reapportionment of State Legislature.

- Fire Department - Minneapolis - Affirmative Action.

- Abortion Issues.

- Mental Health Standards.

- Private cause of actions under Securities law. - Medical Society fee setting involving. While sitting on the Court of Appeals he dissented from an opinion. He would have found the fee schedule violated anti-trust laws. The U.S. Supreme Court reversed the Court of Appeals and adopted his dissent as the law.

- Due Process in Intercollegiate athletics.

P. 70. *St. Paul Pioneer Press*:

1967, Judge Rules Police Acted Improperly.

July 26, 1967, St. Paul Men Acquitted in Smut Trial.

June 25, 1971, Judge Denies Plea in Test of War.

July 22, 1971, Judge Bars Draftee from Vietnam Duty until
Appeal Heard. Minn. 1971 session hours, Chapter 120,
Section 3.

Perkins v. Laird 4-71-Civ-261 (D. Minn. June 25, 1971) Affirmed 17-
1491 ad. 71-1380 (8th Cir. 1971) 7/25/99 -Interview with Judge Larson

P. 72. *U.S. v. Samborski,* 4-68 Crim 65, August 18, 1968

P. 72. *U.S. v. Suchy,* 4-68 Crim 56, September 3, 1968

P. 73. *U.S. v. Hansen,* 4-69 Crim 79, December 19, 1969-314 F. Supp.
91.

The 9th Circuit took the same facts and arrived at the opposite
legal conclusion in opposition to the Geary position. *Parott v. U.S.,* 370
F. 2d 388 (9th Cir. 1966) "An average man of average intelligence, who
can read, must daily realize that he may, once the subject to draft call
from his board due to his designated classification, be 'soon' called
upon to kill."

It is interesting to note that Judge Larson does not discuss the
distinction between "opening the file" and determining if the file should
be reopened because of a "change of circumstance." In this case the
board did nothing. Their only possible defense for this action was that
the defendant had already refused induction. One would expect Judge
Larson to respond to that argument.

P. 74. *U.S. v. Kerwin,* 4-69 Crim 96,313 F. Supp. 791, April 27, 1970

P. 74. *U.S. v. Ready,* 4-70 Crim 32, August 6, 1970

P. 75. *U.S. v. Young,* 4-70 Crim 33,324 F. Supp. 33, October 1, 1970

Both *Kerwin* and *Ready* were handled by experienced capable
counsel. Kerwin was represented by Francis Helgeson, an experienced
senior trial attorney who handled a good number of Vietnam era draft
cases. *Ready* was represented by Chester Bruvold who represented a
major number of the early resisters and successfully marshaled
Gutkneckt and *Kolden* through the United States Supreme Court.

P. 76. *U.S. v. Kelly,* 337 F. Supp. 865,4-71 Crim 284 (January 26, 1972).

P. 76. *U.S. v. Godfrey,* 346 F. Supp. 671,4-72 Crim 170 (August 10,
1972)

In *Kelly* the court did find Mr. Kelly not guilty of a separate count of refusal to report and submit to a physical because the order for the physical did not comply with the regulations.

P. 76. *U.S. v. McGee*, 402 U.S. 479 (1971)

P. 77. *Joseph v. U.S.*, 405 U.S. 1006 (March 27, 1972)

P. 77. *Fein v. Selective Service*, 405 U.S. 365 (March 21, 1972)

P. 77. *U.S. v. Jones*, 4-71 Crim 256 (April 4, 1972)

P. 78. *U.S. v. Hruska*, 4-72 Crim 20 (April 7, 1972)

P. 79. *U.S. v. Olmscheid*, 4-71 Crim 253,350 F. Supp. 889 (April 20, 1972). Olmscheid also presented a fairly common situation in that he filed a C.O. application after his other claim was denied and he received an induction order. The question of whether or not his C.O. application was properly before the board turned on the question of whether or not he should have been granted the prior classification request.

P. 79. *U.S. v. Boone*, 4-72 Crim 157 (August 14, 1972)

Pp. 79-80. *U.S. v. Leavenworth*, 4-72 Crim 29 (August 1, 1973)

P. 80. *U.S. v. Carlson*, 4-73 Crim 128 (November 20, 1973)

P. 80. *U.S. v. Boucher*, 4-74 Crim 48 (May 22, 1974) Reversed 509 F.2d 991 (January 23, 1975) In *Boucher*, Judge Larson relied upon the decision in *U.S. v. Alarik* 439 F.2d 1349 (8th Cir. 1971) as rejecting a selective prosecution argument similar to the Boucher evidence. In *Alarik* we did produce evidence of discrimination based on age, but the crime of aiding and abetting non-registration was arguable different from the act of non-registration by a person whose age required registration. No such difference exist in the Boucher case.

P. 80-81 In both *Carson* and *Boucher* on Judge Larson relied on Judge Neville's decision in *U.S. v. Klotz* 4-73 Crim 130 (1973), Rev. 500 F.2d. 580. Rehearing denied 503 F .2d 1056.

P. 82. Judge Neville found due process problems in *U.S. v. Wallen* 4-70 Crim 34, 325 F. Supp 34 July 2, 1970 and *Selttenbaugh v. Tarr* 4-70 Civil 512 426 F. Supp. 180 January 19, 1991. On identical facts J. Larson found no due process problem in *U.S. v. Young* 4-70 Crim 33,

324 F. Supp 69 October 1, 1970, *U.S. v. Smith* 4- 70 Crim 148, March 2, 1971, and *U.S. v. Treichler* 6-70 Crim 80, January 16, 1971.

Other Decisions by Judge Larson as follows:

> *U. S. v. Titerrud,* 4-69 Crim 11, September 12, 1969.
>
> *U.S. v. Anderson,* 4-69 Crim 93, December 15, 1969.
>
> *U.S. v. Nelson,* 4-69 Cim 5, July 3, 1969.
>
> *U.S. v. Geary,* 368 F. 2d 144 (2nd Cir. 1966).
>
> *U.S. v. Scarlet,* 4-70 Crim 121, September 1, 1970.
>
> *U.S. v. Thielman,* 4-69 Crim 76, April 20, 1970.
>
> *U.S. v. Evans,* 4-69 Crim 82, March 20, 1970.
>
> *U.S. v. Gresham,* 4-69 Crim 87, June 6, 1970.
>
> *U.S. v. Smith,* 4-70 Crim 13, November 6, 1970 affirmed 465 F. 2d 388 (CA 8th 1972).
>
> *U.S. v. Nass,* 4-70 Crim 51, May 11, 1970.
>
> *U.S. v. Treichler,* 4-70 Crim 80 (January 15, 1971).
>
> *U.S. v. Sandstad,* 4-70 Crim 149 (April20, 1971).

In Sandstad we argued that Judge Larson should not back away from his decision in *Kerwin* and *Murray v. Blatchford.* We also argued that we fully met the amended criteria for an opening in fact set forth in *Jasperson & Ready* both quoting Judge Lord in *U.S. v. Schmidt,* 4-70 Crim 17 (December 1970).

> *U.S. v. Kerwin,* 4-69 Crim 96,313 F. Supp. 1300 (April 1, 1969).
>
> *Murray v. Blatchford,* 307 F. Supp. 1038 (D.R.I. 1969).
>
> *U.S. v. Jasperson,* 4-70 Crim 178 (December 1971).
>
> *U.S. v. Ready* 4-70 Crim 32 (December 1971).
>
> *U.S. v. Hanson,* 460 U.S. 337 (8th Cir., May 16, 1972).
>
> *U.S. v. Strandguist,* 345 F. Supp. 217, 4-72 Crim 123 (July 14, 1972).
>
> *U.S. v. Turk,* 4-72 Crim 106 (August 14, 1972) -Was very similar to Strandquist with the same result.

In the following cases after *Ready,* Judge Larson convicted defendants who filed C.O. applications after they received an order to report for induction. *U.S. v. Miels,* 4-70 Crim 142, May 28, 1971.

U.S. v. Treichler, 4-70 Crim 80, June 15, 1971.

U.S. v. Bazevic, 4-71 Crim 233, December 28, 1971.

U.S. v. Becker, 4-71 Crim 249, April 7, 1972.

U.S. v. Sandstad, 4-70 Crim 149, April 29, 1972.

U.S. v. Gimmestad, 4-72 Crim 52, June 15, 1972.

U.S. v. Sharp, 4-72 Crim 84, June 23, 1972.

U.S. v. Skogsberg, 4-72 Crim 104, July 21, 1972.

Mention should be made of the 1970 decisions by Judge Larson in *Shor* and *Smith*. Shor was one of the first persons indicted in 1968. He was an active resister whose induction was accelerated because he turned his card in. After the reversal in Gutknecht the case came back to Judge Larson on a motion to vacate the prior finding of guilty. The government opposed the motion. It wanted to reopen the case and offer evidence that Shor would have been inducted anyway. Judge Larson refused the request. In *Smith* it does not appear that the defendant had any serious claim to a requested hardship classification.

U.S. v. Shor, 4-68 Crim 8 (April 9, 1970)

U.S. v. Smith, 4-71 Crim 148 (March 2, 1971)

Chapter Seven
Judge Philip Neville

Pp. 85-86. *United States v. David Gutknecht* 2-72 Crim 17 - June 30, 1972. Sentence reduced on motion, October 31, 1972. The affidavit given to the court in this case was also made a part of the sentence reduction motion for Mathew Hoffman, which resulted in reducing Hoffman's sentence from 24 to 18 months. 283 F. Supp. 945 (D. Minn. 1968),406 F. 2d 494 (8th Cir.-1969). 396. U.S. 295 (1970).

As a result of *Gutknecht,* the national office recruited lawyers for national and state headquarters and reserve judges advocate officers to work with the case histories. They also set up a new procedure by appointing lawyers in each of the six regions of the nation to check each file before it was sent to the U.S. Attorney for indictment.

P. 88. *In Service of Their Country*, Dr. Willard Gaylin. Viking Press (1970). Judge Neville was dismissive of each of these arguments. As to the parole considerations, it "is beyond its jurisdiction." As to Reach-Out, he stated that the defendant could have had "essentially equivalent treatment by accepting alternative service originally, but he steadfastly has refused to do so."

I to do not intend to "argue" or contend with Judge Neville in any manner, yet I must point out, that as to "support" we never mentioned finances. It was "aid, comfort and support" we had in mind. In the motion for the sentence reduction to Judge Thomas in Mark Hoffman's case, I submitted the same affidavit showing current year sentences which I submitted to Judge Neville. Hoffman's sentence was reduced to 18 months. *Who's Who in Minnesota 1964*

P. 89. *U.S. v. Jensen*, 337 F. Supp. 13,4-71 Crim 36, sentence reduction January 4, 1972.

P. 89. Sentences in Selective Service and Income Tax Cases. The Honorable Gus J. Solomon. 52 F.R.D. 481.

P. 89. *St. Paul Pioneer Press:*

>May 5, 1967, "Philip Neville Nominated for Judgeship"
>August 5, 1967, "For Philip Neville, Federal Judgeship
>Completes Full Circle of Law."
>February 14, 1974, "District Judge Neville Dies."

P. 89. *Minneapolis Tribune:*

>February 14, 1974, "Leukemia Kills District Judge Neville."

P. 89. *New York Times:*

>February 16, 1974, "Philip Neville, 64, U.S. District Judge."

P. 90. Interview with Alan Weinblatt, October 26, 1999.

P. 90. Interview with Thor Anderson - July 28, 1999

P. 91. Kenneth Tilsen personal legal file concerning David Gutknecht.

P. 91. The Selective Service cases tried to Judge Neville by the writer before September 22 and the results are as follows:

Duane T. Wallen - 4- 70 Crim 34, 315 F. Supp. 34 (July 2, 1970) - Not Guilty.

Randahl Segal - 4-71 Crim 73, (March 26, 1971) - Not Guilty.

Ralph Crowder - 4-71 Crim 37, 332 F. Supp. 251 (Sept. 2, 1971) - Not Guilty.

Lon R. Button - 4-71 Crim 123,330 F. Supp. 123 (Sept. 2, 1971) - Guilty.

Francis J. Wieners - 4-71 Crim 127, (Nov. 10, 1971) - Guilty. 6 months-prison plus 18 months probation w/18 month required CO type work.

James Jannetta - 4-71 Crim 242,342 F. Supp. 500, (April 3, 1972) - Not Guilty.

John Filter - 4-72 Crim 42, (July 19, 1972) - Not Guilty.

In addition to the matters discussed in the body of the case I sat as a court appointed stand-by counsel in a draft case involving a religious fundamentalist. *U.S. v. Daniel Tapio,* 4-71 Crim 246, (July, 1972). I had a very limited role as Mr. Tapio had a religious advisor who spoke to the Lord each night and gave the court the benefit of those communications. One could not help but be impressed with the Judge's consideration and patience.

Pp. 91-93. The Northfield 88 was legally entitled as *United States v. Ellen Beard,* et al. - 4 - 70-CRIM-103. The trial team included Minneapolis attorneys Larry Leventhal, Dag Grudem, Robert Aim and John Stout. Larry Leventhal practices law in Minneapolis. He is a widely recognized expert in Indian Law and part of the defense team in the nine-month St. Paul trial of Dennis Banks and Russell Means arising out of the stand-off at Wounded Knee in 1973.

P. 93. *Minneapolis Tribune*
June 12, 1970. "Senate Rejects Further Use of U.S. Troops in Cambodia."

P. 94. *U.S. v. Nelson,* 4-69 Crim 006, 299 F. Supp. 300, May 12, 1969
U.S. v. Schneider, 3-68 Crim 059, 294 F. Supp. 805, September 8, 1969.

P. 95. *U.S. v. Crocker,* 3-68 Crim 51, May 17, 1970, 420 F. 2d 307. (8th Cir. 1971).

P. 95. *U.S. v. Drombroski*, 4-70 Crim 57, July 23, 1970, 445 F. 2d 1289 (8th Cir. 1971).

P. 96. *Wright v. Selective Service System*, 5-70 Civil 58, 319 F. Supp. 509 (October 5, 1970) 444 F. 2d 83 (8th Cir. 1971) - *Wright*, a civil case is not reflected in the appendix.

Pp. 96-97. *U.S. v. Wallen*, 4-70 Crim 34, 315 F. Supp. 459, July 2, 1970.

P. 97. *U.S. v. Young*, 4-70 Crim 33, 324 F. Supp. 69, October 1, 1970.

P. 97. *Slettenbaugh v. Curtis Tau, et al.*, 4-70 Civil 512, 422 F. Supp. 180 (January 19, 1971).

P. 98. *U.S. v. Treichler*, 6-70 Crim 80, January 16, 1971.

P. 98. *Slettenbaugh* like *Wright* is a civil case and not reflected in the appendix.

P. 98. *Oestereich v. Local Board No. 11*, 393 U.S. 238 (1968).

P. 98. *Bream v. Selective Service Local Board No. 16*, 396 U.S. 4609 (1970).

Pp. 98-99. Interview with Brian Solem.

Pp. 98-99. *U.S. v. Anderson*, 4-70 Crim 20, June 9, 1970.

P. 99. We do note that apparently Judge Larson also rejected the argument in one other case. The Appellate Court noted the issue briefly citing *Young* and not *Wallen*.

U.S. v. Smith, 465 F. 2d 388 (8th Cir. 1972).

It does not appear that *Wallen* was widely followed but no case was found except *Young* and *Treichler* that disapproved.

U.S. v. Wolosezuk, 328 F. Supp. 696 (D. Mass. 1971) - found *Wallen* not applicable because board did grant a classification change.

U.S. v. Ford, 306 F. Supp. 42 (D. NH 1970) Reversed on other grounds, 431 F. 2d 1310 (lst Cir. 1970).

U.S. v. Steiner, 460 F.2d 760 (5th Cir. 1972).

I do not want to leave the impression that *Wallen* or any other case reflected or caused disharmony between Judges Neville and Larson. I have every reason to believe that the opposite is true. That is, Judge Neville and Judge Larson had respect and admiration for each other without regard to these or any other disagreements.

Pp. 100-102. *U.S. v. Kroncke and Therriault*, 5-70 Crim 19 (March 12, 1971)

P. 103. *U.S. v. Crowder*, 4-71 Crim 37, 332 F. Supp. 251 (September 3, 1971).

P. 103. *U.S. v. Trepp*, 4-71 Crim 124,332 F. Supp. 1331 (October 22, 1971).

P. 103. *U.S. v. Levin*, 5-70 Crim 21,326 F. Supp. 1069 (March 29, 1971).

P. 104. *U.S. v. Crocker*, 3-68 Crim 51 (March 18, 1969, sentenced reduced May 17, 1970).

P. 104. *U.S. v. Dombroski*, 4-70 Crim 57 - Dombroski also received a six-month sentence for burning his papers at the time of his pre-induction physical but that six months was "concurrent with the two year sentence.

P. 104. *U.S. v. Yule*, 4-69 Crim 055. The docket sheet shows my name as attorney for Mr. Yule. It is stricken and first one and then another attorney was appointed for Mr. Yule. I have no file or recollection of the case. I spoke to friends of Yule who described him as a very simple young man who could not intellectualize his positions—and a man who had a very difficult time in prison.

P. 104. *U.S. v. Doyscher*, 4-71 Crim 324 (April 12, 1972).

P. 105. *U.S. v. Jensen*, 4-71 Crim 36, 337 F. Supp. 13 (January 4, 1972).

P. 105. "Sentences in Selective Service and Income Tax Cases." Judge Solomon 52 F.R.D. 481 (May 8, 1970).

P. 106. *U.S. v. Dooley*, 4-71 Crim 334, transcript of hearing May 4, 1972. Mr. Dooley originally plead guilty. Prior to sentencing he brought a motion to withdraw his guilty plea which was denied. An appeal was taken from that order and affirmed. *U.S. v. Dooley* 471 F.2d 570 (8th Cir., January 5, 1973) In April of 1973 a motion was made to reduce the sentence. Judge Neville reduced the sentence from six months to forty days, but it is unclear if it was simply a clarification of the remaining jail time after service of the balance.

P. 107. *U.S. v. Gutknecht*, 2-72 Crim 17 (June 30, 1972, sentence reduced October 31, 1972).

P. 109. *U.S. v. Jannetta,* 342 F. Supp. 500, 4-71 Crim 242 (April 3, 1972).

P. 109. *U.S. v. Erickson,* 5-73 Crim 10 (July 10, 1973) In *Erickson* Judge Neville cited *U.S. v. Augustine* 4-70 Crim 74 (D. Minn. 1971) *U.S. v. Bergstrom* 5-70 Crim 20 (D. Minn. 1971) *U.S. v. Kelly* 473 F.2d 1225 (9th Cir., 1973) *U.S. v. Walsh* 279 F. Supp. 115 (D. Mass. 1958).

P. 109. *U.S. v. Dozark,* 2-72 Crim 179 (July 26, 1973).

P. 110. *U.S. v. Leistiko,* 346 F. Supp. 27, 4-72 Crim 113 (August 1, 1972).

P. 110. *U.S. v. Lang,* 4-71 Crim 339 (April 17, 1972).

P. 111. *U.S. v. Lewis,* 3-72 Crim 66 (July 20, 1972).

The following additional cases were decided by Judge Neville:

> *U.S. v. Seaman,* 4-68 Crim 84, January 30, 1970.
>
> *U.S. v. Clark,* 470 Crim 12, July 19, 1970.
>
> *U.S. v. Heck,* 4-70 Crim 88, July 22, 1970.
>
> *U.S. v. Yule,* 4-69 Crim 55, March 20, 1970.
>
> *U.S. v. Haack,* 4-70 Crim 8, July 15, 1970.
>
> *U.S. v. Lee,* 3-70 Crim 42,315 F. Supp. 422, July 16, 1970 (Dismissed January 24, 1972).
>
> *U.S. v. Murray,* 4-70 Crim 83, 335 F. Supp. 792 (October 7, 1970). Aff. 452 F. 2d 503 Cert. Denied.
>
> *U.S. v. Ehlert,* 402 U.S. 99, June 21, 1971.
>
> *U.S. v. Kjeld-Olufschwabe Hansen,* 4-69 Crim 42,337 F. Supp. 1090 (August 8, 1971).
>
> *U.S. v. Gorder,* 4-69 Crim 73, 332 F. Supp. 1403 (October 4, 1971).
>
> *U.S. v. Speed,* 4-70 Crim 151, (February 19, 1971).
>
> *U.S. v. Johnson,* 4-70 Crim 191 (April 27, 1971).
>
> *U.S. v. Larson,* 4-70 Crim 16, (April 30, 1971).
>
> *U.S. v. Kardell,* 4-71 Crim 36,336 F. Supp. 1022 (December 29, 1971).
>
> *U.S. v. Button,* 4-71 Crim 123,330 F. Supp. 849 (September 2, 1971).

U.S. v. Gutknecht, 2-72 Crim 17 (June 30, 1972, sentence reduced October 31, 1972).

U.S. v. Higbee, 3-72 Crim 15 (September 12, 1972).

U.S. v. Hanson, 460 F.2d 337 (8th Cir. 1972).

U.S. v. Broyles, 423 F.2d 1229 (4th Cir. 1970).

U.S. v. Peterson, 456 F.2d 1099 (8th Cir. 1972).

U.S. v. Iverson, 455 4.2d 79 (8th Cir. 1972).

U.S. v. Newmann, 4-71 Crim 255 (July 18, 1972).

Chapter Eight
Denouncement

P. 113. *Sentences in Selective Service and Income Tax Cases 52* Federal Rules Decisions 481 (See Appendix)

P. 116. Federal Sentencing Manual-2000 Edition. The current guidlines for sentencing in the Federal Courts became effective in 1987. Sec 2M4.1 covers *Evasion of Military Service.* The severity is a base level "6" unless the offence occurred at a time when persons were being inducted for compulsory service in which case it is a "12." A base level 6 calls for probation with no time served. A base level 12 (or ten if there is a Guilty plea) could be ten to sixteen months in prison, but a ten-month sentence could be served five months in jail with work release and fivemonths of electronic monitoring.

To Do Justice

P. 122. Learned Hand, The Spirit of Liberty: Papers and Addresses of Learned Hand.

I remember once I was with [Justice Oliver Wendell Holmes]; it was a Saturday when the Court was to confer. . . . When we got down to the Capitol, I wanted to provoke a response, so as he walked off, I said to him: "Well, sir, goodbye. Do justice!" He turned quite sharply and he said: . . . "That is not my job. My job is to play the game according to the rules." 306-7

Judge Hand commented that "I have tried to follow, though oftentimes 1 found 1 didn't know what the rules were. Id at 307.

P. 123. *Minneapolis Tribune*, 9/26/2000 "Federal Judge dismisses plea agreement in Gangelhoff case.

St. Paul Pioneer Press, 9/26/2000 "Gangelhoff Plea Deal Tossed Out.

P. 124. *Minneapolis Tribune*, 11/19/98 - "New Trial Ordered for Man Facing 90 Years in Prison." Phillip Robertson case 97 Crim 147 (D. Minn.).

P. 124. *St. Paul Pioneer Press*, 1/20/2001 "Judge Quits Case Over Sentencing" Shellie Landmade case.

P 125. *State of Minnesota v. Prabhudail*, 602 N.W.2d 413 (Minn. Ct. App. 1999).

P. 126. 68 Columbia L.R. 1003 (1968) Robert Cover reviewing *Atrocious Judges: Lives of Judge Infamous as Tools of Tyrants and Instruments of Oppression.*

Justice Accused Anti-Slavery and the Judicial Process. Robert M. Cover Yale University Press (1975.)

Acknowledgments

This book was made possible by a grant from the Minnesota Historical Society and the support of the Hamline University School of Law that provided space, support personnel, and student assistants through the kind offices of Dean Edwin Butterfoss and Associate Dean William E. Martin.

Throughout the several years of research and writing, there were many people who provided inspiration, motivation, and assistance.

At the Minnesota Historical Society Debra Miller, Ann Regan, and Tracey Baker along with others were of great help. At the law school, the work of Vickie Jauret, administrator of the law school Clinic and Lawyering Skills programs made the task of writing this book possible. Professor Howard Vogel's observations and critiques of early drafts were invaluable as was the general support and comments of Professors Angela McCaffrey, Joe Daly, Richard Oakes, Marie Fallinger, David Corbin, and Peter Thompson. Susan Kieffer, director of the law school library and other library personnel were omnipresent in their assistance. In particular, John Tessner, head of services, was tireless in responding to my daily requests in the early stages of my research. My student assistants, May Lee and Shirin Botros, were diligent and a pleasure to work with.

Frank Dorsal, Clerk of Court for the United States District Court for the District of Minnesota, was particularly helpful as were all of the assistant clerks in Minneapolis and St. Paul. In recovering documents from the Federal Depository in Chicago I had the invaluable help of my granddaughter, Kimberly Tilsen.

I wish to thank all of the persons who agreed to be interviewed including, Judge Earl Larson, Judge Miles Lord, Magistrate Judge Earl Cudd, Judge Thor Anderson, Alan Weinblatt, Peter Thompson, David Pence, Judge Laurence Baskir, Dan Scott, Scott Tilsen, Mark Wernick, Fran Shor, Fran Galt, Dave Gutknecht, and Don Olson. In addition to being interviewed, Don Olson spent days with me in the newspaper archives at the library digging out the records of the antiwar movement in Minnesota. His encyclopedic knowledge of the movement substantially eased our task. He also commented on the first draft of the book, as did Dave Gutknecht, who applied his knowledge of the events, insight, and understanding and his skills as an editor to correct and comment in great detail on every subsequent draft.

Many others offered advice and encouragement or served as readers, John Sayers, John Lind, Jeannie Brookins, Ron Amincade, Peter Ratchleff, Ross McMillian, Len Cavise, Susan Kaplan, Peter Carroll, Greg Gout, and Don Irish each played an invaluable role. Finally, this book could not have been completed without the loving support and assistance of Connie Goldman and my family, David, Joci, Judy, Dan, and Mark. Lastly I wish to thank North Star Press and Corinne and Seal Dwyer for their skill, attention, and commitment to this project. I apologize to the many who helped me whom I did not acknowledge. I am appreciative of each, and to each a heartfelt **Thank You.**

Appendix

Contents of Appendix

A. All Judges 189

    1) Summary of Adjudications and Indictments 189

    2) Mean Sentence in Months 190

    3) Cases Tried to Court, Guilty Plea and Jail Sentences 191

    4) Number of Persons Sentenced Each Year 192

B. Equivalency Score—"E"-Score 193

C. Judge Lord 195

    1) Detail of Decisions 195

    2) Sentencing Details 196

    3) Bar Graph—Adjudicated Cases over Time 197

    4) Line Graph—Mean Sentences in Months

        and Sentences Adjusted to Equivalency Model 198

D. Judge Devitt 199

    1) Detail of Decisions 199

    2) Sentencing Details 200

    3) Bar Graph—Adjudicated Cases Over Time 201

4) Line Graph–Mean Sentence in Months
and Sentences Adjusted to Equivalency Model 202

E. Judge Larson 203
1) Detail of Decisions 203
2) Sentencing Details 204
3) Bar Graph–Adjudicated Cases Over Time 205
4) Line Graph–Mean Sentence in Months
and Sentences Adjusted to Equivalency Model 206

F. Judge Neville 207
1) Detail of Decisions 207
2) Sentencing Details 208
3) Bar Graph–Adjudicated Cases Over Time 209
4) Line Graph–Mean Sentence in Months
and Sentences Adjusted to Equivalency Model 210

G. *U.S. v. Gutknecht*–Affidavit of Kenneth E. Tilsen 211

H. *U.S. v. Gutknecht*–Order on Motion to Reduce
Sentence–Judge Neville 215

I. Sentences in Selective Service and Income Tax Cases–
by Judge Gus J. Solomon 221

- A -

All Judges

Summary of Adjudications and Indictments

Tried to court:	Guilty:	131	Dismissed:		
	Not guilty:	85	Complied:		
			Failed Physical:	43	
Jury:	Guilty:	26	Accepted C.O.:	6	
	Not guilty:	1		123	
Pleas:		85	Dismissed:		
			Dismissed by U.S. Attorney[1]:		
Total adjudicated:		328	Without Stating Reason:		271
	Entered Service:	74	Illegal Board Order:		8
			Arrest Warrant Not Served[2]:	48	
				327	

Total dismissed: 450

Total in study: 778

[1]Substantially all of the dismissals in this category are cases in which the Assistent U.S. Attorney found the case unwinnable after indictment because of changes in the law or local board errors. As a matter of practice, the U.S. Attorneys did not show in the record the reason for the dismissal unless the defendant complied.

[2]These cases consist substantially of defendants who left the country.

Mean Sentence in Months: 1970 to 1974
(Equivalency Model Minus Minnesota Eight)

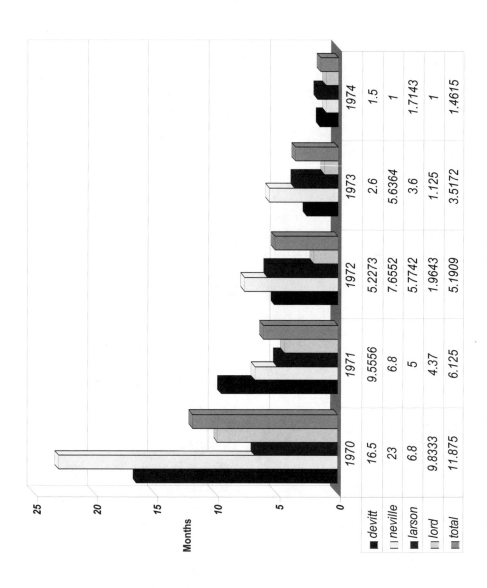

	1970	1971	1972	1973	1974
devitt	16.5	9.5556	5.2273	2.6	1.5
neville	23	6.8	7.6552	5.6364	1
larson	6.8	5	5.7742	3.6	1.7143
lord	9.8333	4.37	1.9643	1.125	1
total	11.875	6.125	5.1909	3.5172	1.4615

Months

	Cases Tried to Court				Guilty Plea		Guilty Court & Jail Sentences				
JUDGE	GUILTY SENT.	NOT GUILTY	TOTAL	% GUILTY	GUILTY PLEA	GUILTY JURY	TOTAL SENTENCED	JAILED	%JAILED	AVE. JAIL SENTENCE	MED.
Devitt	31	11	42	74%	10	11	[1]52	[1]23	46	[1]27.3	[1]24
Neville	32	25	57	56%	18	9	[2]59	50	84	[2]9.88	6
Larson	50	19	69	72%	27	0	77	28	37.7	9.57	6
Lord	18	29	47	38%	30	6	54	7	13	10.86	6

[1]Judge Devitt's record is distorted by five-year sentences given to five defendants known as the "Minnesota-8" who were convicted of attempting to destroy Selective Service records. If these cases were removed, his percent jail becomes 38.6%, his average jail sentence 18.22 months, and his median sentence twelve months.

[2]Judge Nevill's record is also distorted by five-year sentences to two members of the "Minnesota-8." If these cases were removed, his average jail sentence would be 7.84 months.

Number of Persons Sentenced Each Year

	1968	1969	1970	1971	1972	1973	1974	1975	1976	Total
Judge Devitt	2	2	9	10	21	5	2	0	1	52
Judge Neville	0	1	4	12	29	12	1	0	0	59
Judge Larson	2	1	10	21	30	5	7	1	0	77
Judge Lord	0	0	6	8	28	8	4	1	0	54
Total	4	4	29	50	111	30	13	1	1	242

- B -

Equivalency Score "E"-Score

The "E"-score is the author's effort to compare the sentencing behavior of the judges in some manner other than looking exclusively at the number and length of jail sentences.

The Equivalency scale; the E-score used throughout this work is as follows:

24 months of probation = one month in prison

12 months of probation with a requirement that the person per form work similar to that of a conscientious objector = one month in prison

Thus for example, a sentence of six months in jail followed by 24 months of probation is equal to seven months in jail. The "score" is simply the result of adding up all sentences and dividing by the number of persons sentenced.

While the E-score itself is not particularly valuable, the methodology permits every sentence to be translated into an equivalency of months in jail and each individual judge's sentencing behavior as well as the sentencing by the court as a whole can be plotted and displayed over the time period. This is done in further charts.

The "E" score for the four judges are as follows:

Judge Devitt - 13.40 - [1]adjusted 8.44
Judge Neville - 9.79 - [2]adjusted 8.03
Judge Larson - 5.27
Judge Lord - 3.03

Some research has been done into equivalency concepts in sentencing primarily relating to sentencing alternatives.

Professors Noral Morris and Michael Tony discuss the problem in *Between Prison and Probation* published by New York Oxford University Press (1990).

In 1994 Joan Petersila and Elizabeth DeSchenes of the Rand Corporation did a study of equivalency utilizing interviews and questionnaires of inmates and guards at the Stillwater prison in Minnesota. (*The Prison Journal,* Vol. 74, No.3, 1994).

I discussed my scale with several judges and a number of defense attorneys and prosecutors. In general, the judges and defense attorneys thought it was about right. At least one former U.S. attorney who prosecuted draft cases felt that no length of probation was equal to any jail time. Several state sentencing guideline bodies have attempted to develop different types of punishment alternatives that would equate a given prison sentence.

In adopting a scale for use in these Selective Service cases, I relied on the knowledge that 100 percent of the defendants had no prior criminal history or life style experience that could serve to make probation an unwelcome option.

The scale adopted remains the informed but nonetheless personal judgment of the author.

---

[1]Judge Devitt's "E" score has been adjusted by removing from consideration five defendants, known as the "Minnesota 8," who were each sentenced by Judge Devitt to five years in prison following convictions for attempting to destroy Selective Service records.

[2]Judge Neville's "E" score has been adjusted by removing from consideration two "Minnesota 8" defendants who he sentenced to five-year prison terms.

- C -

Judge Lord

Total Adjudicated: 84	Guilty:	Not Guilty:
	Court: 18	Court: 29
	Jury: 6	Jury: 1
	Plea: 30	—————
Total sentenced:	54	30

Sentencing Details:

Jail:	Probation after Jail	
24 mo: - 2	24 months after 6 mo. jail -	1
12 mo: - 1	22 months after 2 mo. jail -	2
6 mo: - 2	18 months after 6 mo. jail -	<u>1</u>
<u>2 mo: - 2</u>		4
7		

Probation without jail

48 months w/out c.o. required -	1
36 months w/out c.o. required -	2
36 months w/24 months c.o. required -	7
24 months w/out c.o. required -	12
24 months w/24 months c.o. required -	9
24 months w/18 months c.o. required -	1
24 months w/6 months c.o. required -	2
24 months w/12 months c.o. required -	7
12 months w/0 months c.o. required -	5
0 months w/0 months c.o. required -	<u>1</u>
	47

Fines

$2000 after 24 months probation -	1
$1500 after 48 months probation -	1
41500 after 24 months probation -	1
$1000 after 24 months probation -	1

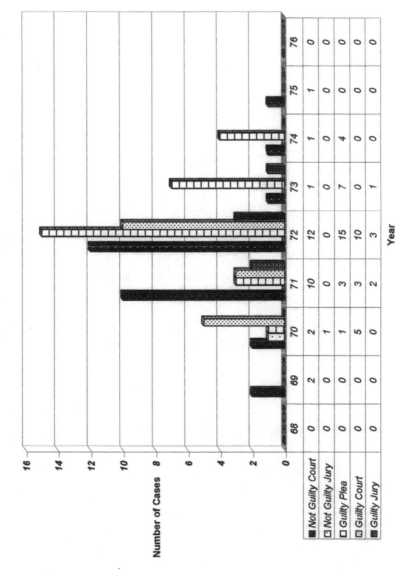

Lord Adjudicated Cases Over Time

	68	69	70	71	72	73	74	75	76
■ Not Guilty Court	0	2	2	10	12	1	1	1	0
▣ Not Guilty Jury	0	0	1	0	0	0	0	0	0
▢ Guilty Plea	0	0	1	3	15	7	4	0	0
▨ Guilty Court	0	0	5	3	10	0	0	0	0
▨ Guilty Jury	0	0	0	2	3	1	0	0	0

Year

Number of Cases

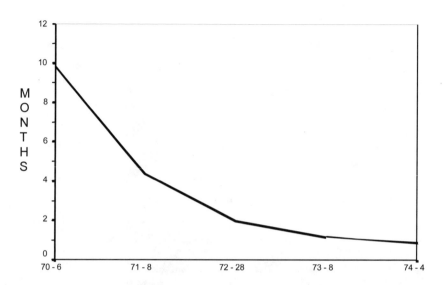

Year of Outcome - Number Sentenced

Sentences Adjusted to equivalency model

24 mo:	2	3 mo:	8
12 mo:	1	2 mo:	23
7 mo:	2	1 mo:	17

Judge Devitt

Total Adjudicated: 63	Guilty:		Not Guilty:	
	Court:	31	Court:	11
	Jury:	11	Jury:	0
	Plea:	10		
Total sentenced:		52		11

Sentencing Details:

Jail:

60 mo:	5
48 mo:	1
36 mo:	2
24 mo:	5
12 mo.	5
6 mo.:	4
4 mo.	1
	23

Probation after Jail

18 mo. after 6 months jail -	4
20 mo. after 4 months jail -	1
	5

Probation without Jail

36 mo. w/36 mo. c.o. required -	1
36 months w/24 months c.o. required -	10
36 months w/0 months c.o. required -	5
30 months w/24 months c.o. required -	1
24 months w/24 months c.o. required -	5
24 months w/18 months c.o. required -	1
24 months w/12 months c.o. required -	1
24 months w/0 months c.o. required -	3
12 months w/12 months c.o. required -	1
12 months w/0 months c.o. required -	1
	29

Fines

$1800 w/36 months probation -	1
$2000 w/36 months probation -	2
$2000 w/24 months probation -	1
$1500 w/36 months probation -	1
$1000 w/18 months probation plus 6 months in jail -	1
	6

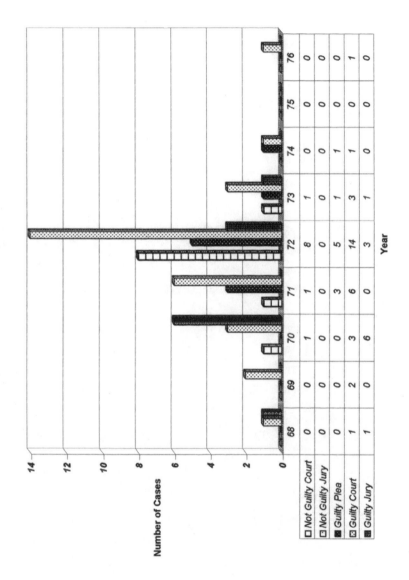

Devitt Adjudicated Cases Over Time

	68	69	70	71	72	73	74	75	76
☐ Not Guilty Court	0	0	1	1	8	1	0	0	0
▨ Not Guilty Jury	0	0	0	0	0	0	0	0	0
■ Guilty Plea	0	0	0	3	5	1	1	0	0
▨ Guilty Court	1	2	3	6	14	3	1	0	1
■ Guilty Jury	1	0	6	0	3	1	0	0	0

Number of Cases

Year

Mean Sentence in Months:

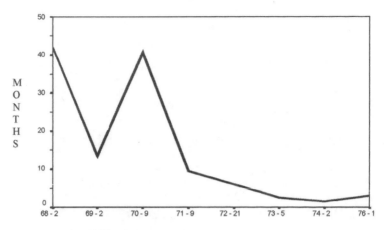

Year of Outcome - Number Sentenced

Sentences Adjusted to Equivalency Model

60 mo:	5	7 mo:	4
48 mo:	1	5 mo:	1
36 mo:	2	3 mo:	12
24 mo:	6	2 mo:	11
12 mo:	4	1 mo:	5

- E -

Judge Larson

Total Adjudicated:	96	Guilty:		Not Guilty:	
		Court:	50	Court:	19
		Jury:	0	Jury:	0
Total sentenced:		Plea:	27		
			77		19

Sentencing Details:

Jail:		Probation after Jail	
24 mo:	4	6 mo. jail 24 months probation	2
18 mo:	3	6 mo. jail 18 months probation	13
12 mo:	1	4 mo. jail 24 months probation	1
6 mo:	17	4 mo. jail 20 months probation	2
4 mo:	3		18
	29		

Probation w/out Jail

48 months w/o months c.o. required -	1
36 months w/36 months c.o. required -	1
36 months w/24 months c.o. required -	20
36 months w/0 months c.o. required -	9
24 months w/24 months c.o. required -	2
24 months w/12 months c.o. required -	1
24 months w/0 months c.o. required -	9
18 months w/12 months c.o. required -	4
12 months w/0 months c.o. required -	1
3 months w/0 months c.o. required -	1
	49

Fines

$2500 w/24 months probation -	1 person
$2000 w/36 months probation -	3 person
$1800 w/36 months probation -	1 person
$1500 w/36 months probation -	3 person
$1500 w/24 months probation -	1 person
$1000 w/48 months probation -	1 person
$500 w/36 months probation plus 24 months c.o. type work required -	2 persons
$500 w/24 months probation -	2 persons
	15

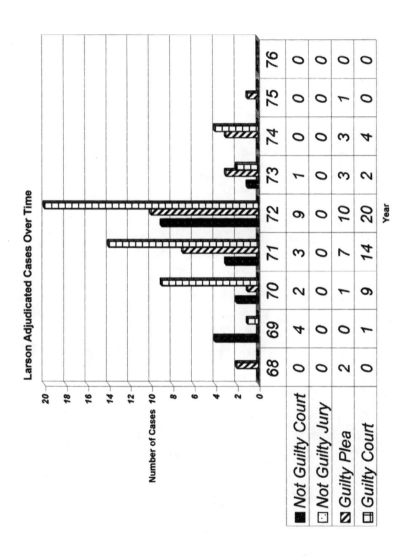

Larson Adjudicated Cases Over Time

	68	69	70	71	72	73	74	75	76
■ Not Guilty Court	0	4	2	3	9	1	0	0	0
☐ Not Guilty Jury	0	0	0	0	0	0	0	0	0
◪ Guilty Plea	2	0	1	7	10	3	3	1	0
⊞ Guilty Court	0	1	9	14	20	2	4	0	0

Year

Mean Sentence in Months:

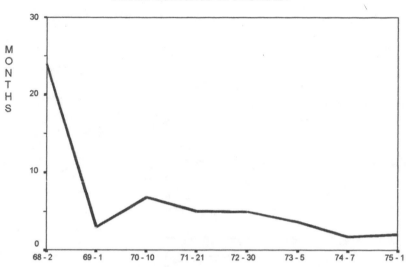

Year of Outcome - Number

Sentences Adjusted to Equivalency Model

24 mo:	4	5 mo:	2
18 mo:	3	3 mo:	20
12 mo:	1	2 mo:	20
7 mo:	16	1 mo:	9
6 mo:	2		

Judge Neville

Total			
Adjudicated: 85	Guilty:		Not Guilty:
	Court: 32		Court: 26
	Jury: 9		Jury: 0
	Plea: 18		
Total sentenced:	59		26

Sentencing Details

Jail:		Probation after Jail	
60 mo:	2	6 mo. jail 24 months probation	
36 mo:	2	& 24 mo. c.o. -	1
24 mo:	2	6 mo. jail 24 months probation -	11
12 mo:	1	4 mo. jail 24 months probation -	2
6 mo:	32	3 mo. jail 21 months probation -	1
4 mo:	5	6 mo. jail 20 months probation -	2
3 mo:	5	4 mo. jail 20 months probation -	3
1 mo:	1	6 mo. jail 18 months probation	
	50	& 18 mo. c.o. -	5
		6 mo. jail 18 months probation -	13
		4 mo. jail 18 months probation -	1
		1 mo. jail 12 months probation	
		& 12 mo. c.o. -	1
		3 mo. jail 10 months probation -	

Probation w/out Jail

36 months w/24 months c.o. required -	3
36 months w/12 months c.o. required -	1
36 months w/0 months c.o. required -	1
24 months w/24 months c.o. required -	1
24 months w/12 months c.o. required -	2
24 months w/0 months c.o. required -	1
	9

Fines: $250 w/ 24 months probation -   1
$1000 w/36 months probation -   1

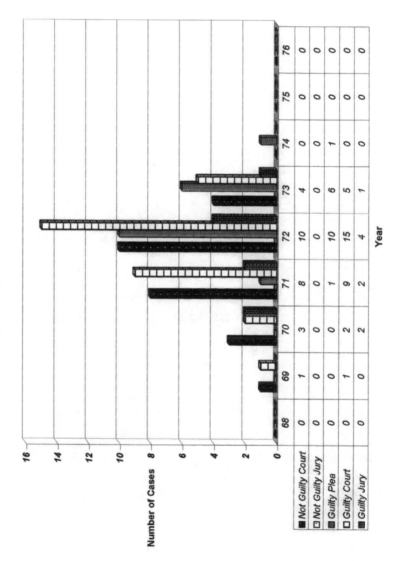

Neville Adjudicated Cases Over Time

	68	69	70	71	72	73	74	75	76
Not Guilty Court	0	1	3	8	10	4	0	0	0
Not Guilty Jury	0	0	0	0	0	0	0	0	0
Guilty Plea	0	0	0	1	10	6	1	0	0
Guilty Court	0	1	2	9	15	5	0	0	0
Guilty Jury	0	0	2	2	4	1	0	0	0

Year

Number of Cases

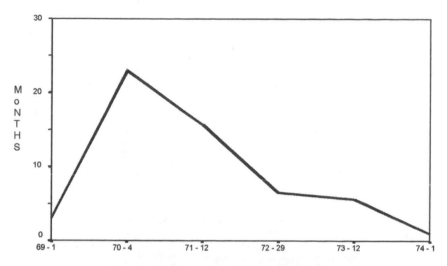

Year of Outcome - Number Sentenced

Sentences Adjusted to Equivalency Model

60 mo:	2	7 mo:	24
36 mo:	1	5 mo:	6
24 mo:	3	4 mo:	2
12 mo:	1	3 mo:	4
8 mo:	8	2 mo:	5

- G -

U.S. v. Gutknecht
Affidavit of Kenneth E. Tilsen

UNITED STATES DISTRICT COURT
DISTRICT OF MINNESOTA
SECOND DISTRICT

United States of America, Plaintiff,
vs. David Earl Gutknecht, Defendant.   No. 2-72 Crim. 17

AFFIDAVIT

STATE OF MINNESOTA)
)   ss.
COUNTY OF RAMSEY)

KENNETH E. TILSEN, being first duly sworn deposes and states that he has made a detailed study in an effort to determine the actual sentences handed out by the United States District Judges for the District of Minnesota in the District of Minnesota for violation of the Selective Service Law.

Affiant has used as his source of information the Minnesota Information Bulletins regularly published by the Minnesota Headquarters of Selective Service System and mailed at regular intervals to the local boards in which the Selective Service System advises the local boards of the result of all cases handled by the Department of Justice. In this connection, affiant has had conversations concerning the data he has accumulated and the method used by the Minnesota headquarters of the Selective Service System in obtaining and reporting the data. These conversations have been with the Director and the Assistant Director of the Selective Service System for the State of Minnesota. Affiant understands that the Assistant Director of Selective Service receives said information from the Office of the United States Attorney and accumulates said data in his office and reports the same to all local boards. Matters such as the present matter are usually not included in the reports until all legal proceedings have ended. Affiant has personally spent considerable time in accumulating this data and alphabetizing all of the names reported in the Selective Service memoranda in order that he could eliminate duplications and correct errors, which duplications have been eliminated and errors corrected wherever possible. In this connection, affiant has personally checked a number of the files in the office of the United States District Court involved. Affiant has also eliminated the one case involved in the reports in which the United States District Court for the District of Minnesota was not involved.

Further, affiant has made an effort to determine where there has been a change in the sentence by the sentencing judge. Four such instances have taken place, all on March 6, 1972, in which one of the judges of the District Court for the State of Minnesota in four separate cases reduced sentences to one year. Affiant has personally examined the docket sheets in those matters. Those sentences are reported hereafter as one-year sentences. Except for the elimination of duplication, the elimination of out-of-state defendants, not sentenced in or by the judges for the District Court for the District of Minnesota and the reductions personally verified, all of the data hereinafter set forth is exactly as reported by the Minnesota Headquarters of the Selective Service System.

The results of the research is as follows:

2 year prison terms	1
1 year prison terms	8
6 months plus probation	20
60 days plus probation	1
90 days plus probation	1
Probation plus fine	10
Probation or suspended sentence	10
TOTAL CASES REPORTED	69

Affiant further wishes to make it clear that all of the cases referred to hereinabove are included in and between the Information Bulletins issued during the calendar year, 1972, by the Minnesota Headquarters of the Selective Service System beginning with the first Information Bulletin entitled, "Information Bulletin Number 1" dated January 14, 1972, and ending with the information bulletin entitled, "Minnesota Information Bulletin #72-48, dated September 15, 1972.

Further affiant states that he is personally acquainted with the one case in which the defendant received a [two]-year sentence (4-71 Cr. 228). Affiant discussed the case with the attorney for the defendant and with the family of the defendant. The defendant in that case, unlike almost all other defendants, did have a significant prior criminal record involving a felony conviction and was not sentenced by a regular judge of the United States District Court for the District of Minnesota. Trial and sentencing in that case took place before a judge from another district who was temporarily sitting in the District of Minnesota.

Kenneth E. Tilsen

U.S. v. Gutknecht
Order on Motion to Reduce Sentence
Judge Neville

UNITED STATES DISTRICT COURT
DISTRICT OF MINNESOTA
SECOND DIVISION

United States of America, Plaintiff,
v.   2-72 CR. 17
David E. Gutknecht, Defendant.   ORDER ON MOTION TO
                                                      REDUCE SENTENCE

Presented to the court at a hearing held on September 22, 1972 at Minneapolis, Minnesota, was a petition by volunteer counsel on behalf of the above named defendant for a reduction of a three-year prison sentence which this court imposed on June 30, 1972, for a willful and knowing violation of 50 App. U.S.C. § 462, failure to report for and submit to alternative service as a conscientious objector as directed by the local draft board under the provisions of the Universal Military Training and Service Act.

Robert G. Renner, United States Attorney, by J. Earl Cudd, Esq., Assistant United States Attorney, appeared for the plaintiff;

Tilsen, Heffernan & Wells, St. Paul, Minnesota, by Kenneth E, Tilsen, Esq., appeared for the defendant.

Defendant is now confined in the Sandstone Federal Correctional Institution and with credit given for the period between the time of his arrest and trial has served approximately six months of his sentence. Counsel urges a number of grounds in support of his reduction motion. He first read to the court a number of obviously solicited or planned letters, all or substantially all addressed to the court but in counsel's possession, bespeaking in various degrees for leniency on behalf of defendant. He devoted some time to relating the fact that defendant's sister is currently suffering from what may well be terminal cancer; that defendant's mother who lives in the Twin Cities is very distraught; and that the defendant is a mainstay of the family and the staff on which his sister and mother would lean. The presentence report, on the other hand, would indicate that from the fall of 1970 to the fall of 1971, defendant worked at part-time janitorial service earning $100 a month and that since early in 1972 he has been involved in a so-called cooperative natural food store at 26th and Bloomington Avenue and estimated his earnings at $75.00 per month. Clear it is therefore that up to the time of his incarceration he was no great financial support to his family. Further, he erstwhile and for some time prior to arrest apparently was not residing at home and not living with his sister or family who now are said to need him so desperately.

The court does have great sympathy for defendant's mother and for his sister who apparently has a terminal condition. The court resents however the attempt of counsel to attach to the court the responsibility for separating defendant from them. The facts are that the defendant was classified I-0 and was given a conscientious objector status. The local draft board recognized his reluctance to fight in Viet Nam and to partake in killing and so accorded him an opportunity for alternate service. His assignment was to the Union Gospel Mission at St. Paul, Minnesota. All he had to do was to report there as directed, where he would have worked perhaps [forty] hours a week, and earned approximately what he had been earning in the past and he could have been the "staff of life" and comfort to his mother and sister which counsel stresses. Seldom it is that any married man or any man with a family is sentenced to jail but what it is as much hardship on them as on him. All the court can say is that those are things a man should think about before he commits an offense, rather than afterwards and then seek leniency on pleas from those who are hurt by his incarceration. These are difficult, disturbing and upsetting considerations but cannot be the basis for a judge's sentencing; otherwise no married or family person will ever go to jail. The court therefore does not believe that counsel's attempt to lay at the court's door the responsibility for separating defendant from his mother and sister has any merit; rather it is his own action.

Defendant's counsel next commented on the fact that defendant is allowed the freedom of the institution at Sandstone, was allowed a furlough to see his sister and is treated with trust and confidence. The court is pleased to hear this and hopes that such continues, and that he will not violate that trust that is placed in him. That, however, does not augur for releasing him from the prison.

Point is made by the government that the indictment in the case was returned January 20, 1972, and that though diligent effort was made by the United States Marshal, defendant could not be found, nor would anyone give accurate information as to his whereabouts until he was arrested by a Federal Marshal on May 9, 1972, while participating in an antiwar demonstration on the University of Minnesota campus. As a witness on the stand at trial defendant as much as admitted that he knew of the indictment but did not want to be arrested and thus did nothing to aid the authorities in locating him. To the probation officer he admitted he attempted to avoid arrest.

Defendant next urges that in recent years in the United States District Court for Minnesota sentences have not been as severe as that imposed on this defendant. The maximum which the court can impose is five years, plus a fine. Some districts impose the maximum in most if not all cases. Counsel has submitted an affidavit showing that only one two-year prison term has been meted in this district in the last two years, though he conveniently omits a two-year sentence by a visiting Judge Thomas with which he was familiar. He finally points out that some [twenty-eight] draft evaders in this district have been placed on probation. So far as this judge is concerned, a number have been given probation who are members of the Jehovah Witness Sect, where they apparently will agree to do alternate service, after conviction "only if God or the court will so order." In the instance at hand, the defendant has resisted completely even the doing of any alternate service, apparently on the theory that to do such would in some way or another recognize respect, honor or admit the existence of a valid draft law.

Argument is made that defendant is not being rehabilitated during his service in prison, that he is not dangerous and that therefore nothing is accomplished by keeping him confined. This court has adopted a philosophy, see *United States v. Jensen*, 337 F. Supp. 13, 14-15 (D. Minn. 1972), where the court stated:

> The court has had difficulty in resolving the problem presented by this case and other similar cases. Defendant is in effect asking this court to sit as a "super draft board" and to determine *de novo* that he is a conscientious objector and deserves the treatment so accorded, i.e., alternative service, even though he never made any such timely claim to his draft board and it thus did not pass thereon. He is saying to the court that he wants the court to do what his draft board did not do and which he never timely asked them to do, and impose the type of sentence which would be the equivalent of what the draft board would have ordered had he made and established his conscientious objector claim. The court does not believe this is its proper function. The court is not unaware that there is an increasing tendency on the part of some judges to place selective service defendants on probation, and the court is not prepared to say that in some instances it would not do the same. Fundamentally, however, the law of Congress remains on the books, is the law, and provides a penalty up to five years plus a fine for its violation. The court did not enact the law and does not believe that it has the right to substitute its judgment for that of Congress as to whether there ought to be such a law and thus fail to enforce it, or make only token obeisance to it. For the court impliedly to say to anyone who concludes to disobey the draft law that he need not

worry for he will merely receive a "slap on the wrist" and will be put on probation, is to weaken law enforcement and the intendment of the law. While the maximum five-year sentence for failure to submit to induction is perhaps not justified except in unusual cases, yet, if the law is to mean something, its enforcement must of necessity involve some inconvenience and hardship to those who chose not to obey it. . . . This court subscribes to the view expressed by Judge Solomon in an article in 52 F.R.D. 481, 486 (1970), that:

> Since they probably would have been placed on probation had they committed any other non- violent crime, are we justified in denying them probation for a Selective Service violation?
>
> I think we are. Even though there are no mandatory minimums, a Judge must respect the objectives of the law which the defendants violated.
>
> . . .
>
> I realize that "some other young man will have to take the defendant's place in the Army," regardless of whether I send the defendant to jail or put him on probation. But I am convinced that many more young men would refuse to comply with the draft laws if they thought that they would get probation even if convicted. They are unhappy about the prospect of being sent to Vietnam, but they prefer the possibility of going to Vietnam over the certainty of prison.

One who consistently, continuously and flagrantly has flaunted the Selective Service law and is placed on probation has an effect on other registrants, the extent of which is of course incapable of exact measurement, many of whom who have gone to Viet Nam or have faced two years in the military.

It is a fact that under 18 U.S.C. § 4202 any defendant becomes eligible to be considered for parole after service of one-third of his sentence. Counsel has submitted an affidavit to the effect that a research of a number of cases shows that the Board of Parole is reluctant to grant parole until the selective service violator has served at least two years and that parole is seldom if ever granted at the time of initial parole eligibility. The court has no direct information on this, since such is beyond its jurisdiction, but deduces the effort apparently is made to equate the period of imprisonment with the two-year period that one would be required to serve as a Selective Service inductee had he obeyed the law.

The court has given a great deal of thought to this case. Counsel has submitted a plan evidencing that an organization, for which this court has a high regard and respect, known as Reachout Today, Inc. will cooperate and aid and assist defendant if he is placed on probation. This is not the answer in a case such as this. Defendant could have had substantially equivalent treatment by accepting alternative service originally, but he steadfastly has refused so to do.

All in all, despite counsel's somewhat abrasive approach and the other considerations above, the court recognizes the United States may be in the waning years of the Selective Service law and may, according to certain current recommendations and suggestions, advert to a volunteer army within a period of a year from now. Also, Selective Service sentences it is clear have been gradually becoming more lenient the country over. Therefore, considering all circumstances and on all of the files, records and proceedings herein,

IT IS ORDERED That defendant's motion for a reduction of sentence be and the same hereby is granted to the extent of a reduction of one year and the sentence heretofore imposed by this court on June 30, 1972 be and the same hereby is reduced to a period of two years in the custody of the Attorney General.

DATED: October 31, 1972.

Philip Neville
United States District Judge

- I -

Sentences in Selective Service and Income Tax Cases

by

THE HONORABLE GUS J. SOLOMON

Chief Judge, United States District Court, District of Oregon

May 8, 1970

A few years ago, I attended a seminar for newly-appointed District Judges. One of the newer Judges complained that his discussion leader had recommended jail time for most income tax violators. He argued that protection of the public and rehabilitation were the only proper bases for confining a defendant. He told me that he had represented many people charged with income tax violations. He did not condone their failure to pay taxes, but he found that most of them were intelligent, able, and public-spirited people. He also told me that civil penalties were so high that he would rarely impose a fine and would never give any jail time to an income tax violator. When I asked him what he would do if the defendant were a lawyer or an accountant, he said he would not treat him any differently. I then asked him. "What do you do in a Selective Service case when the defendant was classified as a conscientious objector, but refused to perform alternative service because of his religious convictions?" I hardly finished my question, when he answered, "I would give him three years; I give all draft evaders three years."

I am happy that we are holding this seminar because I am concerned about the wide disparity in the sentences imposed for Selective Service violations, and to a lesser extent, for income tax violations. This disparity exists not only among districts, but also within districts.

I know that much of this disparity is inevitable. The sentence that a Judge gives in a particular case depends upon many things: his experience, his background, and his attitudes. There is one Judge in this circuit who believes that next to murder the most serious offense is the failure to pay income taxes on time. Another Judge has a reputation for being lenient toward criminal defendants unless they are charged with Selective Service violations.

I realize that sweeping generalizations are always dangerous, but from the statistics I have seen, I have concluded that most sentencing judges make no distinction on the nature of the violation or on the propensities of the defendant in either income tax or Selective Service cases.

In my twenty years on the court, I have sentenced many income tax violators and many more Selective Service violators. I am still troubled about my sentences. For reasons that I will discuss later, I have decided to order jail or prison sentences for most tax evaders and for most Selective Service violators.

I believe that tax frauds, particularly when committed by lawyers and accountants, are morally reprehensible; that tax evasion is as serious if not more serious than draft evasion; and yet I have concluded that I must impose longer sentences on Selective Service violators than on income tax violators.

In discussing income tax violators, I do not refer to gangsters or racketeers who are convicted of income tax violations because of the difficulties of convicting them for the crimes which provide the source of the unreported income. In Selective Service cases, I do not include those who deliberately injure people, burn buildings, or destroy property in their attempt to discredit our government and who are also guilty of Selective Service violations.

Modern theories of penology encourage us to treat the criminal and not the crime; treatment must be suited to a defendant's individual needs; the retributive concept is cruel, harsh, and outmoded. How does this apply in Selective Service cases? Many of these young men are idealists, with good backgrounds and excellent educations. They have been influenced

> By respected public figures—senators, congressmen, and other people
> who hold high political and military office;
> By presidents of great and respected universities;
> By well-known scientists, scholars, writers and church leaders;

all of whom say that our participation in the Vietnam war is unjust, immoral, and illegal. Many of these prominent people also say that the draft laws are unfair, immoral, and illegal.

We take these promising young men and, upon their conviction as Selective Service violators, we send them to penitentiaries to serve sentences up to five years. We know that they will have to serve a much greater percentage of their terms as violators of the Selective Service laws than they would have had to serve had they been convicted of the Dyer Act or theft of a government check or had they been convicted of larceny or embezzlement of funds belonging to the Post Office or a national bank.

The ABA's "Standards Relating to Sentencing Alternatives and Procedures" recommends that "a sentence not involving total confinement is to be preferred in the absence of affirmative reasons to the contrary." It lists three categories of offenses justifying total confinement:

First: Confinement is necessary in order to protect the public from further criminal activity by the defendant;

Second: The defendant is in need of correctional treatment which can most effectively be provided if he is placed in total confinement; and

Third: It would unduly depreciate the seriousness of the offense to impose a sentence other than total confinement. On the other
hand, community hostility to the defendant is not a legitimate basis for
imposing a sentence of total confinement.

The first two categories are self-explanatory. They do not refer
to either the income tax or Selective Service violators about whom I am
talking.

The income tax violator is usually a business or professional
man in a medium or higher income bracket. He is ordinarily a law-abiding citizen with middle class values in all things except in the area of
income taxes. The recidivism rate is minimal. A great number of the
Selective Service violators are idealistic young men of conscience, who
are opposed to violence. In more peaceful times, they would be among
our most law-abiding citizens.

The third category calls for confinement when other treatment
"would unduly depreciate the seriousness of the offense." This refers
primarily to crimes like forcible rape, extortion and kidnapping—shocking crimes which are morally reprehensible. Even if a court finds that it
is highly unlikely that the perpetrator of the offense will ever commit
another crime and the defendant does not need psychiatric treatment,
the court would be justified in imposing total confinement because of
the nature of the offense.

I do not know whether the authors of the report intended to include income tax and Selective Service violators in this category.
Usually, Category 3 is reserved for acts which are morally bad.

Unfortunately, many bar associations do not regard either the
failure to file or the filing of false returns as a crime involving moral
turpitude. The District Court of Oregon does. But the Oregon State
Bar and the Supreme Court of Oregon take a different view. While the
Supreme Court usually disbars or suspends a lawyer who was given a jail
or prison sentence for a federal income tax conviction, I know of only
one case in which an Oregon lawyer failed to be reinstated after he has
completed his penitentiary sentence for an income tax fraud. Lawyers

who are disbarred for ambulance chasing or for embezzling clients' money are not so fortunate. Apparently it is less reprehensible to cheat the government than to cheat a client. I have heard that the Bar Associations in our neighboring states are even more lenient on lawyers who are convicted of income tax offenses.

The medical societies treat their errant members about the same way.

I suggest another category or sub-category that does include income tax and Selective Service violators. I would call it "'Confinement as an instrument of social control,'" or simply, "Confinement as a deterrent to others."

The federal government raises the major portion of its revenues through income taxes. The income tax is one of the few types of taxes based upon the self-assessment system. Its success depends upon the willingness of citizens to honestly, fairly, and promptly file income tax returns.

When a person is charged with an income tax violation, mere publicity of the offense is a form of punishment because it produces in the offender a feeling of shame and social disgrace. Conviction adds to that feeling. It is not necessary to send the defendant to jail to convince him that he did wrong; he is already convinced.

I believe it is necessary to impose jail sentences upon these defendants as a warning to others that unless they pay their taxes, they may get the same treatment. This is particularly true if the defendants are well-known persons of respectability and high social status. You can feel sorry for a friend who was convicted of income tax fraud, but you can relate his situation to your own better if he got a jail sentence. The impact is greater. We know that the Department of Justice recommends jail sentences in practically every income tax case. A recent memorandum prepared by the Chief of the Criminal Section of its Tax Division supports the Department's conclusion that when prison sentences are imposed, the number of infractions of the revenue laws will be reduced.

In the State of Washington, defendants were sentenced to some jail time in 76–85 percent of the income tax cases during the last fifteen years. Even though Washington's population grew twenty percent and its federal tax collections increased by 400 percent, there has been a steady decline in convictions.

I believe that jail terms should be imposed in most cases, and the more prominent the individual the more compelling the reasons for jail time. I say jail time because I believe that a jail sentence of sixty or ninety days will usually have the same general deterrent effect as a prison sentence. There are occasions when I believe it is appropriate to also fine the defendant.

In our court, if a Judge believes that he may place a business or professional man on probation for an income tax violation, he is expected to discuss it with his colleagues. That does not mean that he will not place a defendant on probation without the approval of his colleagues. The sentencing judge retains the absolute right to do it, but during the past ten years we have had few disagreements, and the three judges in our district like the rule.

Deterrence is the most important consideration in the sentencing of Selective Service violators.

Our government has determined that the draft is the only feasible method of meeting our military manpower needs. The Army relies in part on volunteers, and the Navy relies entirely on volunteers. Each of these services estimates that one-half of its volunteers are draft motivated, and all of the services believe that they could not fill their quotas without the draft.

Americans have become unhappy with our participation in the Southeast Asian War. This is particularly true of young people. They are frightened and worried about themselves, their future, and the world in which we live. Their worries are exacerbated by what they hear and see over the radio and television. They are distressed by the poverty and racism in our cities. They are affected by demonstrations on college campuses against the military and for more meaningful participation of young people in their quest for a better and more peaceful world. They are shocked by the horrible pictures of death and destruction in Vietnam.

The young people are subjected to propaganda against the draft from organizations, some of which hide their sinister character by lofty slogans. They are also subjected to pressures from well-meaning and high-minded friends and relatives.

I am not surprised that many young men violate the draft laws. They appear before us because they have either pleaded guilty or been found guilty of having refused to:

(a) register; or

(b) report for a physical examination; or

(c) report for induction; or

(d) report for alternative service after having been classified as a conscientious objector.

Except for the last group, who are primarily Jehovah's Witnesses, a majority of the others are not religious. They are motivated by ethical, philosophical, or political considerations.

Assuming they are sincere, have no prior records, and have engaged in no violent acts, should they all receive similar sentences?

Since they probably would have been placed on probation had they committed any other non-violent crime, are we justified in denying them probation for a Selective Service violation?

I think we are. Even though there are no mandatory minimums, a Judge must respect the objectives of the law which the defendants violated.

Unlike the usual income tax violator, a Selective service violator does not experience any feelings of shame or regret. There is no stigma attached to detection and conviction. He will not lose the respect or friendship of his peer group. In fact, he probably will be treated as a hero—a man of courage and conscience.

I realize that "some other young man will have to take the defendant's place in the Army," regardless of whether I send the defendant to jail or put him on probation. But I am convinced that many more young men would refuse to comply with the draft laws if they thought that they would get probation even if convicted. They are unhappy about the prospect of being sent to Vietnam, but they prefer the possibility of going to Vietnam over the certainty of prison.

Recently, the *New York Post* carried a short review on a book about war resisters in prisons. The review was entitled, "Go West, CO's (to Oregon)." The reviewer said that of thirty-three Selective Serive violators convicted in Oregon, eighteen were put on probation; but in Southern Texas, of sixteen convicted, none was put on probation. In Oregon, not a single man was given a sentence over three years, but in Southern Texas, fourteen out of sixteen were given five-year sentences, and in Southern Mississippi every defendant was given the maximum.

The reference to defendants placed on probation needs some explanation. The great majority are Jehovah's Witnesses who were classified as conscientious objectors. They refused to report for alternative service because they regard the Selective Service as an arm of the military. To perform work directed by the military would compromise their religious convictions.

A few years ago, I stumbled onto the idea that Jehovah's Witnesses would do alternative service if I ordered it because I am not in military. Romans XIII teaches that the orders of those in civil authority are equivalent to the orders of God.

I know that Selective Service is happy about this solution, and a number of courts throughout the county are using the same technique.

I occasionally give probation in other draft cases, but they usually involve special circumstances. If a defendant is not placed on probation, how does one determine the length of sentence that should be imposed? Should all violators get the same amount of time?

Should the ordinary student be given the same sentence as a student body president or the editor of the college newspaper?

What about the young man who doesn't report for induction because he is personally opposed to the war, but has never attempted to influence anyone else? Should he be given the same sentence as a militant resister—the young man who makes speeches, passes out leaflets, and marches in parades?

Isn't the militant entitled to exercise his constitutional rights to express his opposition to the war, just like his United States Senator, without subjecting himself to additional penalties?

These are difficult problems. I have wrestled with them for a number of years, and I have changed my mind many times. At present, I believe that since the primary purpose of sentencing Selective Service violators is to deter others, longer sentences should be imposed on those violators who occupy prominent positions in student and anti-draft organizations. I intend to sentences of two years.

For the follower, I would impose a sentence of eighteen months, or in the alternative two years, with the requirement that the defendant spend six months in a jail-type institution and the balance of the time in civilian work of national importance.

I believe that these sentences are adequate to carry out the purposes of the law.

Because of the events of the past few days, I desire to add few comments.

I believe that harsher sentences will have the opposite effect. We are interested in reaching the moderates—the middle group who are amenable to reason. The upheavals on campuses all over the country during the past few days point up the danger of polarization.

The problems of unrest and civil disobedience will not be solved by the courts alone. The underlying causes must be removed. Turmoil and unrest will probably continue until after peace is restored.

Both the far left and the far right have skilled agitators who are dedicated to the destruction of our government. Harsh sentences which shock the moderates will make them more receptive to the extremists. This is what we must attempt to avoid.

Selected Bibiography

After Vietnam: Legacies of a Lost War, edited by Charles E. New, John
Hopkins University Press, 2000.

An American Ordeal: The Antiwar Movement of the Vietnam Era,
DeBenedetti and Hatfield, Syracusc University Press, 1990.

A Polemic Against the American Judiciary (Book review of *Atrocious
Judges: Lives of Judges Infamous as Tools of Tyrants and
Instruments of Oppression,* by Richard Hildreth: New York,
1856), Robert Cover, 68 Columbia Law Review 1003,1856.

*Between Prison and Probation: Intermediate Punishments in a
National Sentencing System,* Norval Morris and Michael Tony,
Oxford University Press, 1990.

Bitter Greetings: The Scandal of the Military Draft, Jean Carper,
Grossman Publishers, 1967.

*Chance and Circumstance: The Draft. the War and the Vietnam
Generation,* Lawrence M. Baskir and William A. Strauss, Vintage
Books Division of Random House, 1978.

*Direct Action: Radical Pacifism from the Union Eight to the Chicago
Seven,* James Tracy, University of Chicago Press, 1996.

The Draft: 1940-1973, George Q. Flynn, University Press of Kansas,
1993.

Ghost Dancing the Law: The Wounded Knee Trials, John William
  Sayer, Harvard University Press, 1997.
A Grand Delusion: Americans Descent into Vietnam, Robert Mann,
  Basic Books, 2001.
Hell No, We Won't Go!: Resisting the Draft During the Vietnam War,
  Sherry Gershon Gottlieb, Viking, 1991.
Hitler's Justice: The Courts of the Third Reich, Ingo Muller, Harvard
  University Press, 1991.
In Service of Their Country: War Resisters in Prison, William Gaylin,
  Viking, 1970.
I Refuse: Memories of a Vietnam War Objector, Donald L. Simmons,
  Broken Rifle Press, 1992.
*Jailed for Peace: The History of American Draft Law Violators, 1658-
  1985,* Stephen M. Kohn, Greenwood Press, 1986.
Justice Accused Anti-Slavery and the Judicial Process, Robert M.
  Cover, Yale University Press, 1975.
Law, Morality and Vietnam: The Peace Militants and the Courts,
  Bauman and Bauman, Indiana University Press, 1974.
Law Without Values: The Life, Work and Legacy of Justice Holmes,
  Albert W, Alschuler, University of Chicago Press. 2000.
Legacies of Vietnam, edited by Lawrence R. Velvel, *The Long Term
  View,* Volume 5, Number 3, Massachusetts School of Law,
  Summer 2000.
Let's End the Draft Mess, George Walton, David McKay Co., 1967.
Little Group of Neighbors: The Selective Service System, Davis and
  Dolbeare, Markham Publishing Company, 1968.
Narrative, Violence and the Law: The Essays of Robert Cover, Robert
  Cover, The University of Michigan Press, 1995.
The New Conscientious Objection: From Sacred to Secular Resistance,
  Charles C. Moskos, John Whiteclay Chambers II, Oxford
  University Press, 1993.
Only Judgment: The Limits of Litigation in Social Change, Ayreh Neier,
  Wesleyan University Press, 1974.

Perceptions of Punishment, Joan Petersilia and Elizabeth Piper Deschenes, Rand, *The Prison Journal,* 1994-306-328, Sage Publications.

The Politics of Law: A Progressive Critique, David Kairys, Pantheon Books, 1982.

Popular Trials, Rhetoric, Mass Media and the Law, Robert Hariman, University of Alabama Press, 1990.

Protestors on Trial, Criminal Justice in the Southern Civil Rights, and Vietnam Antiwar Movements, Steven E. Barkan, Rutgers University Press, 1985.

Pursuit of Equity: Who Should Serve When Not All Serve, National Advisory Commission on the Draft (Marshall Commission) Executive Order, 11289, July 1967.

Reconciliation after Vietnam: A Program of Relief for Vietnam-era Draft and Military Offenders, Lawrence M. Baskir and William A. Strauss, University of Notre Dame Press, 1977.

Sunshine Patriots: Punishment and the Vietnam Offender, G. David Curry, University of Notre Dame Press, 1985.

Undeclared War and Civil Disobedience: The American System in Crisis, Lawrence Velvet, University Press of Cambridge, Massachusetts, The Dunellen Company, 1970.

Unquestioning Obedience to the President: The ACLU Case Against the Illegal War in Vietnam, Friedman & Newborne, 1972.

Who Spoke Up: American-Protest Against the War in Vietnam, 1963-1975, Nancy Zaroulis and Gerald Sullivan, Doubleday & Company, 1984.

Working Class War: American Combat Soldiers and Vietnam, Christian Appy, University of North Carolina Press, 1993.

Wrong Man in Uniform: Our Unfair and Obsolete Draft and How We Can Replace It, Bruce Chapman, Trident Press, 1967.

Index

Alarik, Scott, 14, 66, 68, 69, 74, 120, 145, 155.

Ali, Muhammad, 26.

Anderson, Michael, 98, 99.

Anderson, Robert E., 101.

Anderson, Judge Thor, 21, 100, 176, 184.

Anderson, Wendel, 19.

Babcock, Donald, 63, 64.

Ball, Ricky Dean, 44.

Banks, Arthur, 36, 37, 163.

Banks, Dennis, 57, 163, 177.

Beaver 55, The, 129, 137.

Bender, David, 61.

Beneke, Brad, 56, 57, 130, 136, 169.

Beneke, Bruce, 136.

Berglund, Harry, 57, 58.

Blackman, Judge Henry, 152.

Bond, Julian, 15, 16, 156.

Bond v. James "Sloppy" Floyd, 155.

Bondhus, Barry, 7.

Bondhus Family, 7, 8, 150.

Boone, Quentin, 79, 80.

Boucher, Ronald, 80-82, 172.

Breen v. Selective Service Local Board 396, 63, 97, 98.

Brewster, Kingston, 25.

Bruvold, Chester, 37, 50, 52, 172.

Burger, Warren, 53.

Burton, Karl, 61, 62.

Bush, George, xix, xx.

Campbell, Douglas, 9.

Carlson, Bruce, 80, 82.

Carlson, Noffilan, 160.

Carlson, Norman, 162.

Carlton College, 74, 90, 138.

Casper, Mike, 139.

Chompsky, Noam, 100.

Clark v. Gabriel, 63, 170.

Clifford, Clark, 101.

Coleman, Nicholas, 20.

Cooperative Grocer magazine, 144.

235

Cover, Robert, xiv, 126, 148, 182.
Coyle, Brian, 40, 58, 146.
Crocker, George, 3, 11-15, 58, 94-96,
   104, 108, 109, 117, 131, 138-140,
   153, 154.
Crocker, Herbert, 14.
Crocker, John, 13, 14, 68, 118, 169.
Crowder, Ralph, 103.

Daschle, Tom, xix.
Davidov, Marv, 101.
DeBenedetti, Charles, 127, 147, 156.
Democratic Farmer Labor Party (DFL),
   8, 70, 150, 156.
Devitt, Judge Edward N., x, 31, 32, 38,
   42, 47-70, 93, 117-120, 149, 164-
   170, 186, 191-193, 196, 201.
Dombroski, James, 3, 94-96, 104, 108,
   116, 146.
Dooley, Ted, 106, 107, 179.
Douglas, Justice, 52, 60.
Doyscher, Robert, 104, 105.
Dozark, Michael, 109, 110.

Eisenhower, President, 53.
Ellsberg, Daniel, 18, 100, 101, 102, 136.
Erickson, Donald, 109.
E-score, 31, 207.

Falk, Richard A. 125, 155.
Federal Jury Practice and Instructions,
   54, 166.
Fellowship for Reconciliation (FOR), 8,
   145.
Fein, Oliver, 63, 64.
Fein v. Selective Service System, 63, 64,
   170, 173.
First National Draft Card Burning, 2.

First Unitarian Society, 6, 8, 13.
Fleischer, Art, xviii.
Fraser, Representative Donald, 15, 71,
   92.
Orville Freeman, 69.
Fulbright, Senator, 16.

Galt, Francis, 7, 8, 144, 145, 150, 151,
   184.
Gaut, Greg, 85.
Gaylin, Dr. Willard, 86, 176.
Gelfand, Howard, 134.
Gilliam, Robert, 10, 150.
Glass, Andrew J., 101.
Godfrey, Phillip, 76, 77.
Gonyer, Randolph, 43.
Gutknecht, David, 2-6, 8-11, 13, 14, 33,
   47, 50-53, 58, 72, 84, 86-89, 91, 94,
   101, 104, 107, 108, 117, 118, 121,
   140, 143, 144, 149, 150, 152, 154,
   159, 166, 175, 176, 184, 210, 213.
Gutknecht, Doug, 4.

Hall, Douglas, 7, 33, 48, 106, 163.
Happy Resistance Day Costume Parade,
   11.
Harris, David, 3, 149.
Hawley, John W., 37, 38.
Hershey, General Lewis B., 6, 22, 24, 25,
   27, 28, 50, 51.
Higbee, James, 111.
Holland, Dan, 4, 11, 12, 14, 41, 42, 95,
   121, 146, 152, 154.
Hooper, Alan, 102.
Holmgren, Cecil, 70.
Hruska, Robert J., 77, 78.
Hunt, William C., 102.
Huntsiger, Jay, 64.

Hussein, Saddam, xx.

Ilse, Robert D., 43.
International Day of Protest, 8.
Iraq, xx, 146.

Janieke, Alfred, 102.
Jannetta, James, 109.
Jasenko, Mark A., 102.
Jensen, Craig, 89, 105.
Johnson, Jeffery G., 64.
Johnson, President Lyndon B., xii, 16, 26, 151.
Jones, Alan, 118.
Jones, Donahue E., 77, 78.

Kelly, Jerry, 172.
Kennedy, President John F., 24, 130.
Kent State, 16.
Kerwin, James, 39, 74, 75.
Kiemele, Rodger, 64.
King, Martin Luther, 10, 16.
Kolden, Rolf, 50, 152, 153.
Rolf Kolden v. Selective Service Local Board No. 4, Beltrami County, Minnesota, 153, 166, 172.
Korb, Lawrence, xix.
Kronke, Francis, 56, 100, 130, 137.
Kronke-Therriault Trial, 56, 98, 130.
Kunstler, William, 37.

Laird, Melvin, 17.
Lang, David, 110, 111.
Larson and Lindquist, 69.
Larson, Judge Earl R., x, 10, 55, 60, 67-82, 96-98, 116, 119, 120-122, 150, 153, 170-175, 178, 179, 184, 187, 191-193, 196, 205.

Lay, Judge Donald, 48, 60.
Leavenworth, James, 79.
Leistiko, Lawrence, 110.
Leventhal, Larry, 37, 163, 165, 177.
LeVander, Harold, 17.
Levin, James, 103, 104.
Lewis, Michael, 111, 112.
Linkow, Peter R., 92.
Lord, Judge Miles W., x, 31-45, 47, 58, 70, 75, 87, 118, 121, 122, 126, 142, 146, 149, 152, 159, 160-162, 164, 174, 177, 184, 189, 191-193, 196, 197, 206.
Lott, Trent, xix.
Lundegaard, Bob, 6, 149, 152, 157.
Lynd, Stoughton, 100, 102.

MacLaughlin, Henry, 71.
Marshall, Burke, 25, 26.
Minneapolis Federation of Teachers, 19.
Minneapolis School Board, 14.
Minnesota Committee to End the War in Vietnam, 8.
Minnesota Dissenting Democrats, 10.
Minnesota Eight, The, 55-59, 85, 91, 100, 104, 117-119, 130, 132-135, 137, 138, 166, 169, 206, 208.
Minnesota Student Association, 15, 133.
Means, Russell, 37, 57, 163, 177.
Mondale, Walter, 15, 16, 71, 119, 156, 157.
Murray, Bruce Edwavy, 99.
Murray v. Blackford, 174.

Neilson, Gordon S., 101.
Nelson, Brian, 93.
Neville, Judge Phillip, x, xii, 31, 32, 55, 56, 68, 72, 81, 82, 85-112, 117-119,

122, 131, 143, 149, 169, 173, 175-177, 180, 188, 191-193, 196, 209, 217.
Nichol, Fred, 58.
Nixon, President Richard, x, 18, 25, 92.
Northern States Power, 138, 140.
Northfield 88, The, 91, 116, 177.

O'Brien, David, 51.
Oestereich, James, 51, 52.
Oestereich v. Selective Service Local Board 393, 166, 170, 178.
Olson, Donald, 4, 10, 56, 57, 130-132, 138, 143, 146, 184.
Olmscheid, Timothy, 61, 79, 168, 173.
Otis, James, 15.

Pence, David, xxii, xxiii, 1-8, 10, 11, 13, 33, 34, 37, 38, 40, 42, 44, 47-51, 60, 118, 121, 122, 134, 140, 141, 142, 149, 152, 164, 165, 184.
Pentagon Papers, 18, 101.
Perkins v. Laird, 170.
Perpich, Rudy, 21.
Peterson, Seth, 50, 59, 152, 166.
Peterson, Terrance, 60, 116.
Pillsbury, 19, 156.
Pope John XXIII, 100, 177.
Prairie Island, 140.
Pursuit of Equity: Who Should Serve When Not All Serve, 26, 158.

Quakers, 12, 50, 59, 131, 138, 169.

Ready, Douglas, 74. 75.
Renner, Robert, 67, 68, 154, 171, 213.
Robinson, 62.
Roda, James E., 62.

Resistance Action Project, 95.
Rosenbaum, 133.
Ross, Judge, 81, 174.
Rustin, Bayard, 6.

Sagedahl, Marvin, 39, 121.
St. Olaf College, 91.
Salem, Phillip, 11.
Samborski, John, 72, 119.
Schaefer, Jerry, 62.
Schmidt, Claude David, 37-39.
Seeger decision, 38.
Selective Service Law Review, 52.
Serman, John, 50.
Severoid, Eric., 70.
Shor, Francis, 2-6, 8, 50, 73, 144, 150, 152, 166, 167, 175, 184.
Silbley, Mulford Q., 9, 11, 12, 169.
Simmons, Peter, 56, 57, 130, 138.
Slettenbough, Richard, 97, 98.
Smith, Russell, 97.
Solomon, Judge Gus J., xiv, 89, 105-107, 113-117, 119, 120, 122, 147, 176, 179, 188, 223.
Spannus, Warren, 19.
Spock, Dr., 13, 152, 153.
Stephenson, Judge, 8.
Stewart, Justice, 52.
Student Nonviolent Coordinating Committee, 14.
Suchy, Mark, 72, 119, 153.

Tarr, Director Curtis, 28, 29, 173.
Taylor, Romeyn, 101.
Therriault, Michael, 56, 100, 131, 137.
Third National Day of Resistance, 10.
Tiger, Mike, 52, 166.
Tilton, William "Bill," 15, 56, 57, 130,

133-138.
Tilsen, Scott, 54, 184.
Treichler, David, 98.
Trepp, John, 103.
Turchick, Charles, 56, 57, 130, 133, 136.
Twin Cities Draft Information Center
(TCDIC), 10-12, 14, 41, 42, 101,
120, 131, 164.

Ulen, Clifton, 56, 130, 133.
Universalist Church, 11, 13, 68, 94, 95.
Universal Military and Training Act of
1951, 24, 213.
U.S. ex rel Arthur Burghardt Banks v. L. R. Putnam, 163.
U.S. v. Alarik, 155, 173.
U.S. v. Anderson, 174, 178.
U.S. v. Babcock, 64, 170.
U.S. v. Ball, 164, 165.
U.S. v. Bencke, 168, 169.
U.S. v. Boone, 172.
U.S. v. Bouche, 80, 81, 173.
U.S. v. Karl E. Burton, 170.
U.S. v. Carson, 80, 173.
U.S. v. Coyle, 40, 164, 169.
U.S. v. George Crocker, 154, 170, 178.
U.S. v. John Crocker, 154, 159.
U.S. v. Ralph Crowder, 175, 179.
U.S. v. Dombroski, 178.
U.S. v. Dooley, 179.
U.S. v. Doyscher, 178.
U.S. v. Dozark, 180.
U.S. v. Ehlert, 99, 180.
U.S. v. Erickson, 109, 180.
U.S. v. Godfrey, 77, 172.
U.S. v. Gonyer, 164, 165.
U.S. v. Gutknecht, 40, 41, 50-53, 60, 88,
121, 149, 164-166, 172, 175, 180,
181, 188.
U.S. v. Timothy Hanson, 174, 181.
U.S. v. Hawley, 38, 163.
U.S. v. Higbee, 179.
U.S. v. Holland, 164.
U.S. v. Hruska, 78, 171, 173.
U.S. v. Huntsiger, 170.
U.S. v. Ilse, 164.
U.S. v. Kelly, 75, 172, 180.
U.S. v. Kerwin, 74, 75, 164, 172, 174.
U.S. v. Kiemele, 170.
U.S. v. Kronke and Thereault, 168, 177.
U.S. v. James Jannetta, 177, 180.
U.S. v. Jensen, 107, 176, 179, 216.
U.S. v. Jeffery G. Johnson, 170, 180.
U.S. v. Jones, 78, 173.
U.S. v. Lang, 180.
U.S. v. Larson, 180.
U.S. v. Leavenworth, 173.
U.S. v. Leistiko, 180.
U.S. v. Levin, 179.
U.S. v. Lewis, 181.
U.S. v. McGee, 76, 173.
U.S. v. Murray, 180.
U.S. v. Nelson, 94, 165, 174, 178.
U.S. v. O'Brien, 50, 166.
U.S. v. Oestereich, 52, 63, 97, 98, 166.
U.S. v. Olmscheid, 173.
U.S. v. Pence, 159, 164, 165.
U.S. v. Peterson, 170, 180.
U.S. v. Ready, 75, 172, 174, 175.
U.S. v. Robinson, 170.
U.S. v. James E. Roda, 170.
U.S. v. Sagedahl, 164.
U.S. v. Samborski, 172.
U.S. v. Schmidt, 75, 164, 174.
U.S. v. Shor, 150, 175.
U.S. v. Slettenbough, 96, 165, 178.

U.S. v. Smith, 174, 175, 178.
U.S. v. Suchy, 170.
U.S. v. Treichler, 98, 174, 175, 178.
U.S. v. Trepp, 179.
U.S. v. Turchick and Tilten and Ulin, 169.
U.S. v. Unnasch, 40, 164.
U.S. v. Wallen, 97, 98, 173, 178, 179.
U.S. v. Stanley E. Willet, 170.
U.S. v. Young, 98, 164, 172, 178.
U.S. v. Yule, 179, 180.
Unnasch, Lyle, 40.

Ventura, Govenor Jesse, xix.
Vietnam Moratorium Day, 14, 15, 156.
Vietnam Summer 1967, 5, 10, 131.
Vinson, Fred, 25.
VISTA, 1, 2, 48.
Vogel, Howard, xiv, 183.

Walbern, Joe, 92.
Wallen, Duane T., 82, 96, 97, 177.
Walter, Sydney, 12, 153, 154.
War Resisters League, 8, 37.
Weinblatt, Alan, 90, 91, 176, 184.
Wellstone, Paul, 91, 139.
Westing, Arthur H., 101.
Westinghouse, 140.
Willet, Stanley E., 65.
Wounded Knee, 37, 57, 162, 163, 169, 177.
Wright, Robert, 96.
Wright v. Selective Service System, 178.

Young, John, 75, 97.
Young, Steven, 39.
Yule, Roger, 104, 179.